D1623040

Alternatives

in

Education

THE ONTARIO INSTITUTE FOR STUDIES IN EDUCATION
FIFTH ANNIVERSARY LECTURES

Edited by BRUCE RUSK

GENERAL PUBLISHING COMPANY LIMITED
TORONTO

ISBN 0–7736–1008–1

Printed in Canada

FOREWORD

The series of lectures contained in this volume was held in the fall of 1970 to celebrate both the opening of the Institute's new building at 252 Bloor Street West and OISE's fifth anniversary. The purpose of the lectures was to explore alternative approaches to education both within and outside the educational system. The lectures were sponsored by the Board of Governors of OISE and the Departments of Adult Education, Applied Psychology, Computer Applications, Curriculum, Educational Administration, Educational Planning, History and Philosophy of Education, Measurement and Evaluation, and Special Education. A lecture given in February 1971 by Jean Vanier has been substituted for a lecture in the series given by Keith Spicer which was not available for publication.

Thanks are due to many people for their assistance in the production of the lectures and this publication: Dr. R. W. B. Jackson, for his encouragement and support; Ross Traub who constituted the lecture series committee; June Armstrong and the Conference Office for attending to all the details of publicity and physical arrangements; Dick Bartrum who performed a fantastic variety of technical feats; Earle Toppings, who looked after editorial details; the many secretaries who worked on transcripts and drafts; and of course, the speakers for their cooperation during their visit to the Institute and in the production of this book.

CONTENTS

ROBERT JACKSON

Director, Ontario Institute for Studies in Education

INTRODUCTION

Forgive me if I begin on a note of pessimism. Even the most optimistic among us must agree that the world of education today is a deeply troubled one. Throughout North America and beyond, criticism of existing systems of education increases in intensity. Schools are under attack for establishing bureaucratic structures that lead to rigidity, impersonality, and a sterile learning environment that simply turns students off. During the past three years, more than 700 independent schools have been founded, in Canada as well as in the United States; teachers, students, and parents are searching desperately for alternatives to the public school systems, frustrated at what they perceive to be regimented schools, unsympathetic administrators, and teachers shackled by the constraints of the system. It is, of course, disturbing to those of my generation to encounter advocates of a *non-school* educational system. Indeed, if one considers the famous reference to the "race between education and catastrophe", the message I get from many of our youth is that we have bet on the wrong horse, that catastrophe is preferable to schooling as we know it today.

In Canada, drastic changes in our educational systems will be required on financial grounds alone. Simply stated, the sort of education we are now providing is proving to be too expensive, particularly postsecondary education at both the undergraduate and graduate levels. In 1957-8, the federal and provincial governments in Canada spent about $3.3 million on aid to full-time university students, including those in graduate schools. Ten years later, the approximate figure for total public-aid expenditures was $93.9 million. Moreover, the number of students at Canadian universities is expected to continue to rise steeply: in 1957, the total number of students was 78,000; by 1966-7 it had jumped to 232,000; and current projections indicate that by the mid 1970s the total will soar to 540,000. By 1980, Canada will probably have about one million students in full-time postsecondary education.

According to the recent report of the Economic Council of Canada, education is now the largest single segment of total government spending in this country. Education costs now exceed $6 billion annually, more than 20 per cent of the total expenditure of governments. In postsecondary education, it has been estimated that government spending — now more than $2 billion a year — will continue to expand until 1975 at about 15 per cent annually in constant dollars, compared with 5 per cent at elementary and secondary levels. Indeed, some economists have forecast that, if present trends continue, expenditures on education will exceed the gross national product by the end of this century, which is of course absurd.

In addition to expressing concern about costs, government officials and taxpayers alike are insisting on the accountability of institutions of higher education — in fact, of institutions at all levels of our school system. When we consider that the Canadian taxpayer supplies more than 85 per cent of the funds for operating and capital expenditures in higher education, it becomes clear that the issue is not *whether* universities should be accountable, but rather *what form* the accountability should take. The backlash against soaring school costs has also led to the beginning of an Ontario taxpayers' revolt against the costs and systems of elementary and secondary education.

On the one hand, the students in our schools are telling us they do not like what we are offering them; and, on the other, the taxpayers are accusing us of extravagance and isolationism. To use a crude parallel, we seem to be paying far too high a price to produce goods that most of our customers would rather not buy. If we were in the business world, bankruptcy would be just around the next corner.

With cost and criticism of our educational systems reaching new highs, our Institute felt that it was fitting and timely to mark its fifth anniversary by sponsoring a lecture series on the theme, Alternatives in Education. We shall probably be confronted with some disconcerting ideas. I should be disappointed if it were otherwise. Obviously, these are not times for self-congratulation and complacency. However, the very fact that we have been able to assemble several distinguished speakers who do have ideas to offer on alternatives to the present educational system is in itself a basis for some degree of optimism. In fact, the current turmoil may herald the approach of a renaissance in education; certainly, there are signs of regeneration in many parts of our educational systems.

Schools, for example, increasingly are being viewed as community resource centers — for the entire community, not just for those in the traditional school-age bracket. At the same time, others are experimenting with the use of the community as the "school". The commissioner of education in New York State, for example, recently advocated an "external degree" program to enable those not enrolled in colleges to earn degrees after obtaining experience in a particular field and completing some independent study. One state college is already offering a liberal studies program that enables anyone over twenty-two to earn a degree through weekend seminars, independent study, state tests, and his own experience. This broadening of opportunities and avenues for further education may reduce costs and make education available to additional sectors of the public.

Such a program is part of a trend away from formalized instruction and towards greater freedom, for students; this, of course, involves increased responsibility. It is quite possible that we shall soon see the end of compulsory school attendance, at least for students of secondary school age and older, and the disappearance of the concept of the school as a custodial care institution. Ivan Illich and his colleague Everett Reimer feel that, in addition to scrapping their custodial function, schools should stop teaching the socially approved values and cease acting as agents of certification for employment and for social roles. They contend that only *cognitive education* belongs legitimately in the school. In proposing alternatives to the present systems, they argue strongly for the redistribution of certain functions of the school to other community agencies.

Technology, so often pictured as a villain in the dramas of modern society, may offer us new means for providing bigger and better educational resources without a drastic increase in costs. The possibility of interaction between man and machine continues to increase, and revolutionary communication techniques, such as the use of laser beams and satellites, promise to speed up movement of information and broaden its accessibility. We hear of the possibility of a world information grid that would make man's entire knowledge available to the world's entire population. The cost of storing huge masses of data in random memory is falling rapidly. The National Science Library in Ottawa, for example, has combined three scientific abstract services in a system that uses 100-word reader-interest profiles for a personalized service. Patrick Suppes holds out the promise of computer alternatives.

At the Institute, we have been encouraged by the results achieved so far in many of our research and development projects: to mention only a few, our studies of learning, projects in early childhood and remedial education, production of multimedia packages and curriculum materials, co-operative efforts with teachers in the individualization of instruction, studies in school system organization, explorations of the needs and methods of the adult learner, and our assistance to children who suffer from learning disabilities.

These and other signs of vitality and imagination lead me to believe that we *can* meet the stiff challenges of educating children and adults in this crazy environment that changes more quickly than ever before in our history. Such inventive thinking is necessary if our youth are to discern the coherence in the complex world around them and relate themselves to its natural order.

I am happy that OISE is able to offer to the public this series of provocative and timely lectures.

NEIL POSTMAN

Professor, Division of English Education, Speech, and Educational Theater, New York University

TELLING IT LIKE IT AIN'T: AN
EXAMINATION OF THE LANGUAGE OF
EDUCATION

Have you ever wondered why, after all the talking and thinking that we educators have done, education is pretty much the same as it was a hundred years ago? For that matter, two hundred years ago? Oh, we've made some changes, to be sure. We teach Spanish and French instead of Latin and Greek, linguistics instead of grammar, set theory instead of arithmetic. We've substituted the letter grade for the birch rod; and we've subdivided children into ninety-seven different tracks instead of teaching all ages and kinds in one small room. But when you consider what our goals are and how grandiose are our hopes and our talk about how to revitalize education — to make the process of learning a dynamic, active, ongoing, and joyful experience — we've made no progress at all. One "new approach" after another holds out promise, and then, when all the shouting dies down, somehow it falls flat. Why?

My view at the moment is that standard-brand school-talk is a major obstacle to our thinking new thoughts about education, and a major factor in our perpetuating old thoughts. I know that some people believe that language is merely a "vehicle" for thought. But, I tend to agree with Wittgenstein, the great linguistic philosopher, who said that language is not only the vehicle for thought: it is also the driver. If you want to get some sense of what that means, imagine that the only numerical system available to you is what we call Roman numerals. Now try to multiply 476 by 87. I think you'll find it impossible to do — unless, of course, you translate the Roman numerals into Arabic numbers. But if you are stuck with Roman numerals, this is a thought or operation you cannot perform. The point is that the language you think in will always limit the kinds of things you can think. And obviously, what you can't think, you can't do.

Standard-brand school-talk is a special language that quite rigidly structures the way we think about school. For instance, school-talk has two different and distinct words — *teaching* and *learning* — for what is essentially a single, transactional process; and, as a consequence, we are led to think of that process in a way that falsifies the reality of it. It simply makes no sense to say that you have taught someone something, but that he didn't learn it. It's like saying, "I sold you something, but you didn't buy it." And yet, you don't have to hang around the teachers' room in any school (especially an elementary school) for very long before you hear such nonsense, usually expressed with great indignation and earnestness: "I taught him that four times and he can't learn it." Not long ago, in fact, William O'Connor, a member of the Boston School Committee, was quoted as saying that there wasn't anything wrong with the Boston schools that better students wouldn't cure. That's the kind of thinking that can only happen when you talk about *teaching* as one thing, and *learning* as something else.

Let's look at some of the other words that keep us chained to present procedures. The first thing you have to recognize is that some of these words are the present procedures. For instance, consider the word *subject*. Everyone seems to agree that school should, as they say, *teach subjects*. Almost everyone agrees that a subject should be *taught* for roughly forty to forty-five minutes a day; and, at least where I come from, that some subjects are *major* and some are *minor;* that subjects are things you can *pass* or *fail;* and that if you *fail* a subject, you must, as they say, *take it again.* Now, I don't know about you, but this kind of talk strikes me as bordering on the insane. I sometimes get the feeling that teachers believe subjects are natural phenomena, and that when the astronauts finally get to Mars, they will discover that Martian schools are divided into departments of Martian, biology, history, and chemistry — all of which will, of course, be *major* subjects.

Not only is a subject not a natural phenomenon, it doesn't even exist anywhere except inside the schools. Edward Land, who invented the polariod Land camera, once commented on this fact by asking, "Where, anywhere in life, is a person given this curious sequence of prepared talks and prepared questions to which the answers are already known?" The answer, of course, is, "Nowhere — except in school."

What is called a *subject* is an entirely arbitrary invention of schools, consisting for the most part of a set of statements about a roughly similar set of situations, most of which happened or were reported in the past. With a few exceptions, like physical education and possibly composition and mathematics, there is really nothing that students must learn how to do in any school subject, beyond memorizing about 65 per cent of the statements provided by the teacher or the textbook. A school subject, such as history, geography, biology, or literature, bears almost no relation whatsoever to what professional historians, geographers, biologists, or literary critics actually do. And therefore, schools have no realistic performance criteria by which to judge the competence of students. Even in those few cases, for instance composition, in which there is some fairly complex skill to be learned, the performance criteria are usually arbitrary because, if you think about it, you will realize that there is no such thing in the real world as a *composition.* No one ever sits down to write a composition, unless he has been assigned to write one by a teacher. People write radio scripts, letters, articles, novels, editorials, graffiti, notes to the milkman, but no one in real life ever writes a composition — or, for that matter, a term paper, or doctoral thesis. That is why teachers invent idiotic criteria by which to grade student papers — 33 per cent for content, 33 per cent for style, and 33 per cent for grammar, spelling, and punctuation.

This is as true in what we call the "advanced" or "professional" schools as it is in the elementary or secondary schools. I happen to work in a school that, nominally, trains teachers. Actually, nothing of the sort takes place. What we do in our school is offer courses; that is, we teach subjects that the state department of education or other certifying agencies require of prospective teachers. Our students do not learn how to do anything, least of all how to help young people to learn, because one never learns how to do anything of significance, I think, in what is called *a course*. In fact, I really doubt that any serious thought is ever given in our school to the question. On what basis would you determine the competence of teachers? To my knowledge, the question has simply never come up. What we talk about is what courses should be given in what subjects. This sort of talk occurs not because we are particularly stupid or vicious people, but because we take for granted the validity of the language of our profession. And that is a very bad mistake, because our lexicon is almost as questionable as it is long.

Consider this list: *subject, course of study, class, class time, free period, syllabus, homework, curriculum, midterm, final, term paper, gifted student, underachiever, probation, pass, fail,* and my all-time favourite — *incomplete.* You know them as well as I, and can probably easily add another twenty or so to the list. Quite often, when I have a conversation with a teacher or college professor, I feel the way one feels in a conversation with a drunk. By that I mean the drunk always wins; and he wins because he establishes the ground rules, including the tone and style of the encounter. What I am getting at is this: if you permit the language of school-talk — such as the terms I've just

mentioned — to go unexamined, you have to end up thinking pretty much what everyone else is thinking, and has
always thought. If a man tells you he is possessed by devils,
and you reply, "Which ones?", you and he may become
friends, but neither of you will go much beyond where you
are. If you reply, "What the hell are devils?", insight then
becomes possible for both of you. So let's consider a little
more standard-brand teacher and student talk, in the interest of keeping ourselves open to doubt about the existence
of devils.

As of this month, what is called the *new term* has just
begun. (It does sound a little like a prison sentence, doesn't
it?) Let me mention some of the more bizarre utterances
that have been directed to me in the past couple of weeks
by what are called *graduate students* during what is called
Registration Week. (Almost all of these students, by the
way, are what we call *teachers* in their own right.) The most
amusing utterance, from my point of view, is this one:
"How much ground do you cover in your course?" This
sentence reflects what I call "The Vince Lombardi Theory
of Education", because the only people, besides teachers,
who are so interested in covering ground are football
coaches. What this sentence means when asked by a student
of a teacher is mostly a mystery. I think it has to do with
how many different kinds of things the teacher plans to
talk about, but I'm not sure. However, it's pretty clear to
me that the metaphor of *covering ground* bears very little
relation to the process of learning, which, as I perceive it, is
almost never a linear progression from point A to point B,
or from the twenty-yard line to the fifty.

Another favorite utterance of students is to ask if I have
high standards in my courses. There is no mystery at all to
this. All they want to know is, is it easy or hard to get As or
Bs? If it's easy, then one is said to have *low standards;* if it's
hard, *high standards.* This, by the way, is an extremely
important question to students, who learned very early that
being what is called *a good student* means getting what are
called *high grades.* Nothing more, nothing less. I think we

all have to face the fact that schools have never developed any standards of intellectual competence that anyone really takes seriously. And this is as true at Harvard College as it is at a junior high school in a ghetto of Brooklyn.

I am sometimes asked by students why they should *take* a certain course. This gives me a good opportunity to test their crap-detecting apparatus.* If the course is something like the Victorian Novel, I will say to them that the Victorian novel *qua* Victorian novel is good in itself (which is the kind of talk people expect from college professors). If they ask me what the hell I'm talking about, I know I've got a live one on my hands. Usually they don't. More often, I get the reply that I've made a good point, and, from one student in particular, that the Victorian novel is certainly worthwhile *per se*.

Once in a while, a student will ask, "How much does the mid-term count?" My answer is "One hundred per cent, and you have just flunked." Now, students don't find that amusing. After all, they have grown accustomed to what may be called the "Cost-Accounting Theory of Education", in which nothing is ever real, let alone worthwhile, unless it is assigned a numerical value. Incidentally, I think that is why, at least in my school, teachers and students really believe that three-point courses are better than two-point courses.

So long as we continue to talk, and therefore to think, in this way — to rely on this vocabulary and these metaphors — our attempts to make significant changes in the schools are doomed to failure. As I suggested at the outset, you can't develop calculus using Roman numerals as your mode of discourse. You need a new language.

Now, in some respects, the schools have attempted to invent a new language, or at least to modify the old, but they have relied, in these efforts at change, solely on the process of addition — grafting new words onto the old lexicon in the hope that the new concepts would somehow

* Chapter 1 of *Teaching as a Subversive Activity* is entitled "Crap Detecting".

revitalize the old procedures. We've added, for example, words and phrases like *learning how to learn, discovery, inquiry, emotional development, behaviors, behavioral objectives, ecology,* to name just a few. By themselves, these words, and the attempts at new perceptions that they represent, can be vital to educational reform. But they won't work if we confine ourselves to grafting them onto the old vocabulary. What has already happened to those concepts is what usually happens in grafting procedures: the new is either rejected by the old and withers away, or the old remakes the new in its own image.

Let's take *ecology,* for example, a word and a concept we're trying very hard, and with good reason, to incorporate into school-talk. Ecology is the interrelations among all the phenomena and processes in physical and social environments. Ecology is also that point of view that allows one to perceive the interrelatedness of things. When we graft ecology onto our current school lexicon, though, only one thing can happen, and it is happening already. We're making ecology into a *subject* and a subject distinct from — that is, not connected with — language, religion, sociology, political science, history, or physical science. Adding ecology to a lexicon whose most cherished word is *subject* is like screwing a light bulb into the wick of a kerosene lamp. It just won't work. And one of the great psychological mysteries of our time is why we are surprised when it doesn't.

Let's take another example. *Behavioral objectives* is a term that's generated a lot of excitement among teachers lately. Its use reflects our dawning awareness that the schools must help children not to recite, but to do the things that their adult lives will require of them. At least that awareness is a start. But then we graft behavioral objectives onto a lexicon whose key words include *curriculum* and *read.* Trying to prepare children for life in the electronic era by programming them for reading skills is like trying to get to Mars in a Chevy Impala. Adding *behavioral objectives* to the *curriculum* is like adding power steering to the Chevy: you may have a better car, but it just won't go far enough. In this case, the Chevy doesn't have the structure to get you where you want to go.

The point is that addition, as a strategy for reforming school-talk and school-thought, is not sufficient. Medicine could make no genuine progress in its attempts to develop germ theory and bacteriology while its lexicon retained the terms *miasma* and *humors of the blood*. Physical chemistry could not evolve a workable theory of combustion while its vocabulary included the word *phlogiston*. Psychology could make no significant advances in its exploration of human behavior so long as its new vocabulary coexisted with the old terms such as *demons, devils,* and *possession.* What progress required in each case — and in countless others in the history of science — was not just the addition of new words, but the subtraction of old ones.

The lexicon of education needs a little of the same radical subtractive surgery. Imagine what new perceptions we might come up with if we simply subtracted from school-talk some of the words that channel our thinking into the same old patterns. Suppose, for example, the words *subject, course, class, syllabus,* and *curriculum* were banished overnight from the vocabulary of teachers. How would the school day be organized? What skills would you want children to learn? How would you decide what kinds of activities should take place? How would you distinguish between *major* and *minor,* important and unimportant, activities? Would you need to? How would you determine which activities a particular child was *ready for?* How would you judge when a student had *finished* with school? How would you determine which teachers should do what? How would you determine who was qualified to teach?

Suppose the term *grades* were subtracted from school-talk. On what basis would you judge the competence of children in various skills and activities? How would you know when a student was ready to move on to more complex and difficult problems? How would you distinguish between simple and complex problems? How would you judge the competence of teachers? How would you know whether a particular teacher or an entire school had *high standards* or *low standards*? On what basis would you group students? How would you know who were the *under-achievers*? the *slow learners*? the *gifted students*? Would you need to know?

Some people, I know, would offer these very questions as an argument for retaining the word *grades* in the lexicon of school-talk. Without grades, they say, these questions are unanswerable. This is, of course, nonsense. We make count-less judgments every day about the performance of people (not to mention products), and we base some very impor-tant decisions on those judgments: "Should I marry this girl? leave this man? make this friendship? invite her to this party? invite him to give this speech? rely on her for that job? promote her? fire her? trust this doctor? change mech-anics? vote for this candidate?" And we do it all (thank God!) without giving, receiving or asking about *grades*. Can you imagine deciding to marry a girl because she got an A in home economics? Or rejecting her because she got a C? The notion strikes us as ludicrous because we know per-fectly well that the word *grades* has about as much cur-rency in real life as the word *unicorns*. Maybe less. Except in school, where, like cataracts on the eyes, it takes all the depth and color out of our perceptions and blinds us to new possibilities. Why not remove *grades* from the lexicon — subtract the word altogether — and see what new insights we could come up with?

It is hard to think or talk for long about creative innova-tions in education without stumbling over, and falling flat on, the biggest obstacle-making word of all, *school*. The word remains the single most powerful reform-retardant in the language of education, largely because we have come to use it as a synonym for education. It is not. *School* is a place, a building, usually centrally located in a community, but shut off from the community by fences, doors, and windows with locks and bars, and signs saying: VISITORS REPORT TO OFFICE. *School* has a sublexicon all its own:

office, classroom, playground, hall, gym, auditorium, library, chalkboard, bells, P.A. system, walls. Education, we like to believe, is a process — dynamic, personal, integrated, continuous, active. But when we call it *school,* the lexicon of school takes over education and forces it into different molds. *Walls:* leave family, community, world outside. *Classrooms:* face front, be quiet, submerge individuality in group homogeneity. *Desks:* sit still. *Books:* sit still, read, believe, be quiet. *Chalkboard:* look, copy, follow instructions. *Paper and pencils:* sit still, listen, take notes. *Bells:* obey. *Halls:* line up, be quiet. *P.A.:* listen, obey.

Suppose we simply subtracted the word *school* and all its subvocabulary from the language of education. Where would the education of the young be conducted? What kinds of activities might take place? How would students be organized? What skills would teachers need? What tasks could they forget about? How would we distinguish between learning and living? between learning and playing? between education and entertainment? between physical education, social education, and emotional education? Would our not knowing the difference make a difference? How would we know if a student were in an academic or vocational program? Would he care? Would we? How would we know whether he was doing science or social studies or language arts or math or psychology or political science at any given moment? And would it matter? What would we do with all those empty buildings, and with all the money we would save on building new ones?

I think you'll get some idea of the power of subtraction in achieving new perspectives on education if you combine it now with the principle of addition. Imagine for a moment that the word *school* and all its sublexicon — such as *phlogiston* and *miasma, devils,* and *unicorns* — had simply vanished from your vocabulary. Now think about learning to learn, inquiry, discovery, social responsibility. What new activities would these words suggest? What new arrangements for education might they make possible? Pretend for a moment that the words *curriculum, course of study, class, grades,* were simply not available to you for talking or thinking about education. What kinds of behavioral objectives might you come up with? What role might they play in education? What kinds of experiences might they suggest we arrange for young people? Imagine, for just one more moment, that *subject* had disappeared from your vocabulary, along with *classrooms* and *walls.* What might ecology mean for education? What might young people do in the way of ecological activities? What experiences would you want to arrange to reinforce their ecological point of view?

Addition and subtraction are two of the most powerful strategies we have for redefining not just the language, but also the process of education. For, as Stokely Carmichael has put it, "He who holds the power to define is master."

However, there is another linguistic strategy that may, in the long run, prove even more productive in generating creative ideas and practices in education. It consists, quite simply, of renaming what we have been referring to as *a problem*, and calling it *the answer.* Thomas Edison reportedly confessed to a friend, shortly before his death, that he could have given the world the light bulb two years earlier than he did. "But would you believe," he said, "that I spent the first eighteen months standing in front of the damn thing shouting into it, 'Hello? Hello? HELLO?' " That story is apocryphal, no doubt. But there is one in the same vein that's quite true. Recently, when the New York Thru-way Authority faced the problem of an excessive number of speed limit violations, it invented a solution that makes so much sense that the guy who came up with it was probably fired. They raised the speed limit.

If the method of problem-solving suggested by those two stories — that is, simply redefining *the problem* as *the answer* — strikes you as a somewhat dubious semantic trick and nothing more, let me remind you that virtually all the revolutionary advances in science resulted from precisely that form of redefinition. For example, astronomers believed for centuries, with Ptolemy, that the universe revolved around the earth, and for centuries they struggled with *the problem* posed by the countless exceptions to the laws they formulated. When Copernicus came along, he studied the situation, and in effect declared that the exceptions were not a *problem,* they were the *answer:* the sun didn't revolve around the earth; the earth revolved around the sun. For hundreds of years, too, early doctors believed that the only way to heal a wound inflicted by a knife or a sword was to place a potion on the tip of the weapon that had done the damage. And for hundreds of years, they struggled to solve *the problem* posed by all the wounds that healed when the weapons weren't treated. Then Paracelsus came along, studied *the problem,* and simply renamed it *the answer:* the body healed itself, and the process was not affected in the least by treating the instrument that caused the wound.

Education has not been so successful in its methods of problem-solving that it can afford to reject an approach that science uses. So let's try it.

One junior high school in New York City tried it in this way. The problem, as in virtually every school in New York, was that large numbers of students simply refused to remain in their classrooms. And, since every classroom had two doors and one teacher, their teachers could not keep them there. As a result, students roamed incessantly through the halls, where they would run and fight and scream. On occasion, this proved dangerous to those in the halls, and almost always distracting to those who were in the classrooms. The "wanderers" were threatened many times, but to no avail. Then, an assistant principal, in one of those intuitive leaps for which scientists (but not usually educators) are famous, saw in *the problem, the answer.* She announced that the school was instituting a radical educational plan, known as "The Open Hall Policy". Among other things, the plan defined staying in the halls as a legitimate educational activity, so long as running, fighting, and screaming were confined to specific corridors where gym teachers were available to offer advice and minimize injuries. As a consequence, a lot of kids stopped wandering in the halls, and those who stayed there usually talked quietly among themselves or with the teachers available there on an informal basis. My last information was that principals from other schools were visiting this school to observe "The Open Hall Policy" in action.

Let's look at some other *problems* in education that might be redefined as *answers*. One that seems to be bothering almost every teachers' union is class size, or student-teacher ratio. Everyone seems to agree that there are just too many students, and too few teachers. Well, that *problem* could easily be an *answer*, and one that might triple the number of teachers in our schools, at no cost whatsoever to the taxpayers, while enriching the education of all students. The solution: let the students be teachers. If you think this idea is flippant, not to be taken seriously, it may be because you're still thinking of teaching and learning as two distinct processes. Bear in mind these points: *(a)* Teaching-learning is a single, transactional process. *(b)* There is considerable evidence that children learn better from other children than they do from adults. *(c)* You probably know from your own experience that one of the best ways to learn something is to try to teach it. Why not, then, have each student from junior high school on spend some part of his school time each year teaching younger students — perhaps those very "subjects" he is having some difficulty with? If each student were assigned to teach reading or math or electronics or science or whatever, to just three younger students, you would accomplish the following: the student-teachers would learn a great deal more than they would otherwise; the younger students would learn a great deal more than they would otherwise; the regular teachers would have more time and energy for creative teaching than they would otherwise. They might also have more time to be teacher-students in their own right.

Here's another set of *problems* that, taken together, becomes an *answer*. Parents and educators are expressing growing concern about the high rate of student failure, especially in ghetto schools. At the same time, the public is pressing for new ways of establishing teacher-accountability. What could be more sensible than to redefine student failure as teacher failure, and to rate the teacher's performance on the basis of his students' performance. After all, the only sane definition of "to teach" is "to enable another to learn". The tests a teacher gives constitute a very specific definition — and it is the teacher's own definition — of what he or she is trying to enable students to learn. When a student fails a test, it can only mean that the teacher failed to teach him what he or she set out to teach. If the class average is 75 per cent, then the teacher's performance was only 75 per cent effective. This answer to the problem of teacher-evaluation could very well be the answer to another *problem* as well: how to determine teachers' salaries. Why not pay a teacher only that percentage of a fixed salary that corresponds to the class average on the tests he or she gave over the year? That *answer* might answer several other problems in education as well: the grading system, for example, would probably vanish overnight. Or the failing student, at least, would become a thing of the past. To date, the most powerful educational argument anyone has mustered against these proposals is the warning of Albert Shanker, the President of the United Federation of Teachers in New York, that, in such a system, teachers would inevitably begin to give their students the answers. But isn't that what they are supposed to do, in our current system of education? Once again, the answer is in the problem.

Another *problem:* according to surveys of student attitudes toward school, students seem to like their major subjects least, and their extracurricular activities most. But in most schools, extracurricular activities are poorly staffed, overcrowded with students, and badly scheduled. Why? Because they must be held after school. *Answer:* make the extracurricular activities the major subjects, and the major subjects extracurricular. Again, I am not being flippant. What do students learn in a formal English class that they would not learn better, and certainly with more motivation, in publishing a weekly student newspaper, or a monthly magazine of student literature? What do they learn in formal science lectures and laboratory drills that they wouldn't learn more effectively in experiments they originate in science clubs? As things stand now, the main difference between extracurricular activities and major subjects is the greater involvement and participation of students in the after-school programs. Isn't that just what we are strivi. g to bring into the classroom during the school day?

Problem: students cheat. *Answer:* cooperation is a virtue, not a vice, and should be rewarded, not punished. If you don't believe it, check the list of corporations and institutions that are spending vast sums of money and time on group interaction and cooperation training for their personnel. What the schools call "cheating", business now prizes as "establishing maximum accessibility to the total information resources of the group."

Problem: students won't read. They're spending all their time with the TV, films, radio, LP records, tape recorder. *Answer:* bring the TV, films, radio, LP records, tape recorder into education — not as audiovisual aids, but as the focus of serious inquiry into the electronic communications media and their effects on our culture. The students in our schools are getting, and will continue to get throughout their lives, a major portion of their information, perceptions, beliefs, and attitudes through the electronic media. We owe them at least some effort to teach the skills they'll have to have, and the questions they'll need to ask, in order to deal intelligently with those media.

Problem — and this is the biggest one of all: the kids just won't come to school anymore; they want to stay out on the streets. New Rochelle, New York, had this problem a few years ago. Parents, teachers, administrators, and students began to talk with one another about "the problem." And what came out was this: the students, many of them, simply did not want to be in school. They wanted to be, in their own words, "where the action was". Where it was, they weren't sure, but one place it wasn't was school. The students wanted to be on the streets. So, let their education take place on the streets, in the community itself where the action was.

This year, New Rochelle organized a hundred students into teams of ten. Each team is led by a teacher, a high school senior, and a lay member of the community. Each team has identified some community problem it wants to solve: an ecological problem, a political one, or one related to crime, drugs, race, or traffic. Their "curriculum" consists of doing whatever they have to do and going wherever it is feasible for them to go in order to find out as much as they can about the problem, and suggest real, authentic, viable solutions to that problem to the appropriate people in the community.

I could go on, but I'm sure you can begin to provide additional applications of this strategy yourself — just as you can apply the principles of subtraction and addition to your own brand of school talk. Give it a try. After all, what can you lose? It's only talk.

Or is it?

VINH BANG

Directeur adjoint, Département de Psychologie,
Ecole de Psychologie et des Sciences de
l'Education, Université de Genève

LA PSYCHOLOGIE DE J. PIAGET ET SES
APPLICATIONS PEDAGOGIQUES

Sans vouloir provoquer une controverse, nous pouvons nous demander, d'une part, ce que la psychologie a apporté à l'éducation en général comme à l'enseignement en particulier, et d'autre part, ce que la pédagogie a pu tirer des données de la psychologie.

Confrontés pour faire le point, psychologues et pédagogues n'arriveront, je le crains, à ne dresser qu'un bilan assez modeste.

Les premiers surpris seront peut-être les psychologues. Ils seront étonnés de voir que l'Ecole n'a su, ou n'a pu que si peu profiter de l'apport de la science psychologique. La psychologie scientifique, dont chacun reconnaît le développement si rapide, si différencié, a-t-elle manqué un de ses buts, celui de servir l'individu et, par voie de conséquence, le social.

Si la psychologie fait son auto-critique, il convient aussi que la pédagogie pose un diagnostic quant à l'Ecole. Pour ma part, le diagnostic ne serait pas très optimiste, et la solution thérapeutique devrait être recherchée en commun.

Dessinons le cadre général des apports de la psychologie à la pédagogie, et dans ce cadre, examinons quelle est et quelle sera l'influence des études piagétiennes sur les systèmes d'enseignement.

"Toute bonne psychologie aboutira à une application" a souligné Piaget. Remarquons d'emblée que cet aboutissement ne va pas de soi. L'orientation d'une psychologie vers une application de ses données n'implique pas non plus que tout psychologue soit un practicien. Il appartient à la psychologie pédagogique de coordonner la recherche fondamentale et la recherche appliquée sur le plan de la recherche, et de fournir sur la plan pratique les données d'une application concrète.

Donnons d'abord un bref aperçu des applications des données de la psychologie à la pédagogie. D'avance, je vous préviens qu'il choquera certains, et je m'en excuse. Toute extrapolation extrême est dangereuse, mais a l'avantage de fournir une vision plus claire et de souligner l'essentiel.

On connaît trois branches de la psychologie qui offrent des possibilités d'application à l'éducation en général:

La psychologie différentielle qui a consacré trop de temps à la recherche des instruments de diagnostic, se contente d'une validation empirique, accepte comme prémisse le produit de l'Ecole ou de l'éducation, ne s'interrogeant même pas sur le pourquoi des différences individuelles pour ne se préoccuper que des conséquences de ces différences individuelles.

La psychologie de l'enfant a dressé des tableaux de comportement de plus en plus complets et dégagé des caractères essentiels; elle a fourni des constats, nuancés peut-être, mais se cantonne dans des interprétations sans pouvoir les dépasser par des explications.

La psychologie de l'affectivité a pu, grâce à des techniques thérapeutiques, servir l'éducation, mais dans une mesure limitée.

Or sa réussite, même limitée, à partir d'un petit nombre de cas individuels, réside dans le fait qu'elle a cherché des causes, et non simplement établi des constats de conflits ou de complexes. Elle a tenté de remonter à la source, à l'origine, pour comprendre et surtout pour expliquer le processus, et ne s'est pas contentée seulement du fait observable.

Si le rééducateur doit analyser les causes pour comprendre les effets, chercher le processus formateur ou déclencheur de l'inadaptation de la conduite pour décider de la forme de la rééducation, pourquoi l'éducateur lui ne fait-il pas siens des mêmes principes?

Il est trop facile de se poser en accusateur. Mais il faut reconnaître le bien-fondé des reproches que l'on adresse á la psychologie différentielle, d'accentuer encore les différences individuelles en parti fabriquées par l'Ecole, au lieu de trouver des solutions pour une meilleure pédagogie non bâtie sur ces différences.

On peut aussi penser que la psychologie de l'enfant a rendu, je dirais plus attrayante, la vision que l'on avait de l'enfant. Phénomène analogue à ce qui s'est passé avec la télévison. La psychologie de l'enfant a cru pouvoir offrir au maître une dimension nouvelle. Mais elle n'a fait qu'apporter l'agrément de la couleur à l'image existante; le maître croit maintenant comprendre l'élève alors qu'il n'a remplacé la vision en noir/blanc que par une vision en couleur.

Quant à la psychothérapie de l'enfant, elle n'est utile qu'à une minorité. Peut-être d'ailleurs, les systèmes d'éducation ont-ils contribué à lui fournir de la clientèle!

Le problème de l'application de la psychologie à l'éducation doit être repensé entièrement. La crise de l'enseignement actuel témoigne de l'urgence d'une intervention.

Qu'a fait la psychologie dans le cadre de l'Ecole? La psychologie appliquée à l'Ecole a cherché jusqu'ici à déceler les cas-problèmes, c'est-à-dire les cas de désadaptation scolaire, à leur fournir une aide psychologique, dans la plupart des cas psychothérapeutique, afin de pouvoir les réintégrer dans le circuit scolaire normal.

La question de savoir si l'Ecole elle, est désadaptée par rapport à l'évolution actuelle n'a jamais été posée.

La psychologie suit l'Ecole et récolte les cas-problèmes; elle fait du "replâtrage". Elle a vu son rôle se réduire à celui d'une infirmerie.

Sa préoccupation: dépanner les cas urgents.

La psychologie appliquée à l'éducation doit se préoccuper davantage du normal, de l'élève normal, de celui qui pose pas de problème immédiat. Ce normal se porte bien, mais qui sait si un jour il ne tombera pas malade, dans certaines circonstances exigeant une adaptation ou dans certaines conditions défavorables à son développement?

Pour ma part, la psychologie pédagogique doit être une science de la prévention. Elle est issue d'une conception nouvelle selon laquelle il faut tirer de la science en général ce qui peut éclairer le pédagogue, et de la science de l'enfant ce que celle-ci est en mesure de nous apprendre sur son développement, et sur les conséquences que l'éducation a sur celui-ci.

Depuis une quinzaine d'années, la psychologie appliquée à l'éducation a essayé de frayer des voies nouvelles. Peut-être dans la recherche de ce que pourrait apporter la psychologie, peut-être aussi dans l'examen critique de ce bilan, certains regards se sont-ils tournés vers la psychologie génétique de Jean Piaget et vers les travaux de l'Ecole de Genève.

Nombreux sont ceux qui s'intéressent aux travaux de Piaget pour en tirer des applications possibles dans l'enseignement. Cela va de l'initiative individuelle d'un chercheur, d'un maître qui voudrait introduire une réforme pédagogique dans sa classe, voire dans son école, jusqu'aux entreprises plus généralisées comme "Nuffield Mathematics Project" appliqué dans un ensemble d'écoles, depuis cinq ans, sur une population scolaire allant de cinq à treize ans.

Tout un nouveau programme et une nouvelle méthode d'application ont été élaborés sur la base des recherches de Piaget sur la genèse du nombre, sur la construction de l'espace, sur le développement des notions géométriques chez l'enfant.

Sur cet ensemble de réalisations, il est utile de faire un certain nombre de remarques. Comme toute transposition de la théorie à la pratique, l'application de la psychologie de Piaget à la pédagogie se heurte aussi à des difficultés de réalisation.

a) En premier lieu, il faut bien distinguer les préoccupa-

psychologie pédagogique qui voudrait contribuer directement à la réforme de l'enseignement.

b) En second lieu, il faut prendre conscience de la nécessité de recherches intermédiaires, entre la recherche théorique et la recherche d'application, pour définir les modalités et les conditions d'une expérimentation pédagogique sur la base des études piagétiennes.

Piaget a créé une méthodologie pour étudier le processus de formation des connaissances et parvenir à une théorie de la connaissance. L'objet d'étude est l'enfant, l'accent étant mis sur la genèse de son développement mental. Ainsi la psychologie de l'enfant revêt une dimension nouvelle, la psychologie génétique. L'apport de Piaget à la science psychologique est d'avoir essayé d'expliquer la genèse de la construction de l'intelligence.

Au départ, pour parvenir à comprendre la genèse de la connaissance, Piaget a choisi d'étudier la logique de l'enfant et comment cette construction se développe. Il croyait pouvoir saisir ce processus à travers le langage.*

Ce n'est que plus tard, en 1947, qu'il a annoncé qu'il avait adopté une nouvelle méthode d'approche: "au lieu d'analyser d'abord les opérations symboliques de la pensée, nous (Piaget) partirons d'opérations effectives et concrètes de l'action elle-même."** C'est une voie nouvelle qu'il trace ainsi à la recherche, dont le but est de comprendre la réflexion, le raisonnement de l'enfant: faire manipuler par l'enfant un certain matériel simple, lui demander de prévoir, d'anticiper le résultat des transformations ainsi que d'expliquer pourquoi un certain résultat a été possible.

En dépit d'une difficulté réelle à suivre le langage piagétien, bien des gens ont été convaincus par la "petite expérience" toute simple, par exemple celle qui consiste à prendre deux verres identiques, à verser dans chacun d'eux

* J. Piaget, *Etudes sur la logique de l'enfant: Le langage et la pensée chez l'enfants* Neuchâtel et Paris: Delachaux et Niestlé, 1923).

** J. Piaget, Avant-propos de la 3me éd. de *Le jugement et le raisonnement chez l'enfant* (Neuchâtel et Paris: Delachaux et Niestlé, 1947).

la même quantité d'eau, à transvaser le contenu d'un des verres dans un troisième, plus large, et à demander à un enfant de cinq ans "si on a toujours la même quantité d'eau dans le verre-témoin et le verre plus large".

Le plan de recherches de Piaget comprend un ensemble de recherches emboîtées, de telle sorte que le résultat de l'une d'elles est à la fois une réponse et le point de départ d'une nouvelle problématique. Mais tout cet ensemble de recherches est orienté vers le même but: tenter d'expliquer la genèse du développement de l'enfant.

C'est en se fondant sur des centaines de recherches faites sur des milliers d'enfants, que Piaget aboutit à décrire et expliquer l'évolution et le développement du "sujet épistémique", c'est-à-dire l'enfant en général. (Ce sujet épistémique n'est ni un enfant en particulier, ni la somme de tous les enfants étudiés, mais l'enfant en général. L'Ecole, elle, a à s'occuper de chacun de ses écoliers en particulier.)

Or, si Piaget a son objectif propre, la psychologie pédagogique, de son côté, se doit d'en définir un qui lui soit propre également. Elle sait et saura se servir des données psychologiques précisées par les travaux de Piaget comme d'instruments mis à sa disposition par ce savant. Malheureusement, il arrive, et même fréquemment, que Piaget soit mal interprété. Nous faisons allusion ici au fait que n'importe qui peut reprendre une des "petites expériences" de Piaget et constater qu'il obtient les résultats prévus. Mais s'il se limite à ces faits d'expériences, l'expérimentateur prouve qu'il n'a pas vraiment compris ce que Piaget a voulu dire.

La richesse des faits observés, depuis les réflexes du nouveau-né jusqu'au raisonnement de l'adolescent, pour ne pas dire de l'adulte lorsqu'il manie la logique propositionnelle de la pensée formelle, donne, à première vue, l'impression que Piaget est facile à comprendre. Le chercheur qui retrouve les mêmes résultats que lui, dans les mêmes conditions d'observation, est tenté de croire qu'il a compris l'auteur et sa théorie.

De là, des psychologues et des pédagogues bien intentionnés s'imaginent pouvoir appliquer les données de la psychologie de Piaget en transposant, sans autre, les techniques de recherche par exemple, sur la genèse du nombre, de la géométrie, de l'espace, du temps etc. . . . et en faisant des exercices destinés aux élèves. Un tel procédé est certainement voué à des échecs à plus ou moins longue échéance. De bonne foi, les maîtres remettront alors les études de Piaget en question, ou, s'ils gardent encore une certaine confiance en lui, lui reprocheront cependant de ne s'être pas occupé de la psychologie appliquée et de ne pas travailler pour l'éducation.

Or, n'oublions pas que la psychologie pédagogique a ses préoccupations propres. L'enfant n'est plus un objet d'étude. La psychologie génétique de Piaget a permis de comprendre l'enfant. Mais la pédagogie intervient en fonction de cette connaissance pour aider, guider sa formation.

Cette reconversion consiste à rendre opérationnelle pour l'éducation en général et l'enseignement en particulier le modèle de développement de l'enfant établi par Piaget.

Les techniques utilisées pour étudier le processus de la pensée ne peuvent être, sans autre, adoptées comme technique d'enseignement.

Les techniques de recherche, le matériel utilisé pour ces investigations sont adaptés à un but précis. Ce but est de provoquer par les transformations de la boule de plasticine en saucisse, en galette, ou le transvasement d'une quantité de liquide dans un verre plus large ou plus effilé que le verre-témoin, par exemple, un conflit entre des indices perceptifs trompeurs de configuration et la cohérence dans la logique des compensations réciproques. Les résultats ont permis à Piaget de décrire un modèle d'équilibration, "la conservation", traduisant un moment du développement dans la genèse de l'évolution mentale.

Le maître doit connaître l'existence de cette étape, car c'est seulement s'il a acquis "la conservation" que l'enfant peut construire les invariants physiques.

Les pédagogues n'ont pas à reprendre les mêmes techniques d'observation pour constater si un enfant a oui ou non la notion de conservation, mais à se demander si l'existence d'une telle notion ne remet pas en cause toute une conception de la pédagogie. Ils sont conduits dès lors à admettre l'existence des structures opératoires sous-jacentes pour chaque niveau de développement dont ils doivent tenir compte. Ne l'ayant pas compris, certains croient bien faire en recourant à un apprentissage systématique de la notion de conservation comme s'il s'agissait d'une notion de grammaire ou d'arithmétique inscrite à un programme scolaire.

De grand maisons d'édition ont essayé de reproduire les techniques de recherches sur la logique élémentaire, les classifications, les sériations, sous forme d'exercices pratiques pour l'apprentissage de la logique mathématique. Elles ont même introduit certaines variantes pour "enrichir" le matériel.

Leur intentions etaient bonnes, mais ils ont fait et feront à Piaget, sans le vouloir, plus de mal que de bien. Je crains qu'un échec ne vienne couronner à plus ou moins brève échéance cette tentative, car il est clair que les éditeurs en question n'ont pas saisi les données profondes de la psychologie génétique et que la "petite expérience" n'est pas une fin en soi. On court ici le risque de voir imputés à la théorie des échecs dont elle n'est pas responsable, mais qui sont dus aux erreurs de ceux qui l'appliquent. . . .

Essayons de penser à la facon dont la psychologie pédagogique doit comprendre la psychologie de Piaget.

Même limités par le cadre d'un exposé, nous pouvons, par exemple à partir uniquement des trois concepts suivants — l'activité du sujet, les stades de développement, et la méthode clinique — émettre déjà quelques réflexions pédagogiques.

Le Concept de l'Activité du Sujet

C'est par son activité propre que l'enfant construit son intelligence. Essentiellement sensori-motrice au départ, cette activité se double d'une activité représentative dans la période de la formation de la fonction sémiotique. L'activité concrète sert ensuite d'appui pour une activité mentale. Le sujet manipule le réel pour interroger le réel. L'activité opératoire le fait anticiper de plus en plus quant à son activité concrète. Enfin l'activité devient essentiellement mentale lorsque l'adolescent manie les opérations du combinatoir sur des données propositionnelles; le comportement ne permet pas à lui seul de saisir le rôle de l'activité du sujet et c'est l'activité mentale de celui-ci qui intéresse la pratique pédagogique. Cette activité apparente dans les conduites du sujet n'est compréhensible pour le maître que lorsque nous pouvons lui expliquer les opérations intellectuelles qui lui sont sous-jacentes et constituent le groupement opératoire selon la formule de Piaget.

L'Ecole active, comme l'Education nouvelle, il y a 50 ans, a mal compris l'idée de "l'activité" de l'élève.

Penser, c'est opérer; opérer est pris ici dans le sens d'une élaboration mentale. A un certain moment du développement, cette élaboration n'est possible que si l'enfant manipule le concret. C'est parce qu'il opère qu'il est actif. Proposer un exercice scolaire est en fait proposer une activité de raisonnement, de réflexion, et de création. Toute activité doit être intégrée dans l'ensemble des activités qui concourent au développement mental. Une telle programmation peut être suggérée par une psychologie de l'apprentissage. Dans cet ordre d'idée, l'Ecole de Genève a entrepris depuis plusieurs années l'étude sur l'apprentissage "opératoire"; les résultats de ces recherches auront une incidence directe sur la pédagogie.

Le Concept de Stade de Développement

Les résultats de certaines recherches parallèles menées dans différents laboratoires de psychologie ne concordent pas nécessairement avec ceux de Genève, quant aux âges correspondants à tel ou tel sous-stade.

Reprenons la définition des stades donnée par Piaget: "les trois conditions nécessaires d'un système de stades sont qu'ils se succèdent en un ordre constant chez tous les sujets, que chacun puisse être caractérisé par une structure d'ensemble (et pas seulement par un caractère dominant) et que ces structures s'intègrent les unes dans les autres selon leur ordre de formation".

L'essentiel pour la pédagogie est de savoir respecter

l'idée d'un ordre de succession constant pour tous, avec le palier formateur indispensable et le palier d'équilibre nécessaire. Le terme stade décrit deux situations dans le langage piagétien: d'une part ce sont les grandes étapes du développement, la période de l'intelligence sensori-motrice, celle des opérations concrètes et enfin celle des opérations formelles; d'autre part, il y a des stades dans la construction de telle ou telle notion, par exemple les stades de la construction du nombre.

La seconde idée que la pratique pédagogique doit respecter est celle de la notion de structure d'ensemble. La construction du nombre ne se fait pas indépendamment de celle de la géométrie, de l'idée du hasard, de la causalité etc. . . . Le dénominateur commun de cette interdépendance est la structure du groupement opératoire sous-jacent.

Il est à remarquer que la pédagogie classique a morcelé la connaissance en disciplines, telles que l'enseignement de la langue, de la grammaire, du vocabulaire, de l'élocution, de la lecture, de la composition, de la dictée etc. . . .

Une réforme partielle semblable à celle de l'enseignement des mathématiques mérite d'être encouragée. Mais une telle entreprise, parce qu'elle n'est pas coordonnée avec d'autres, risque de commettre la même erreur que la psychologie associationniste qui soutenait l'idée d'une association des facultés mentales prises isolément.

C'est pourquoi la recherche d'applications doit s'inscrire dans un plan d'ensemble.

La Méthode Clinique

Si nous voulons souligner ce troisième point, bien qu'il ne s'agisse pas là d'un des concepts de la théorie du développement psychogénétique, mais au départ une méthode d'investigation adoptée par Piaget pour étudier les processus de raisonnement chez l'enfant, c'est parce que nous élaborons maintenant une pédagogie clinique.

Cette didactique permet de respecter à la fois les différences individuelles, non dans l'optique de la psychologie différentielle qui s'intéresse aux performances, mais dans celle d'une pédagogie qui s'adapte au processus du cheminement de la pensée de l'élève vers l'assimilation d'une notion. Que des individus différents aient réussi une même performance ne signifie nullement qu'ils ont mobilisé les mêmes représentations, opéré sur le réel avec les mêmes démarches, adopté les mêmes stratégies de résolution.

C'est par l'étude de ces différences individuelles que nous pouvons appréhender aussi la créativité, un sujet de recherche très actuelle en pédagogie.

La didactique clinique serait ainsi un dépassement de la didactique opératoire parce qu'elle coordonne la dimension génétique avec les différences individuelles.

La question à examiner maintenant, c'est celle des conditions nécessaires pour que la psychologie génétique de Piaget ait un impact sur une pédagogie donnée.

a) Pour ma part, la première démarche à entreprendre est de rendre opérationnelles, en terrain pédagogique, les données de la psychologie piagétienne.

Cette démarche ne pourra aboutir que par la constitution d'un organe de recherches intermédiaires, recherches qui, pour la facilité du discours, sont dénommées recherches en psychologie pédagogique.

Ces recherches ne sont pas fondées uniquement ou exclusivement sur la théorie de Piaget. Elles s'appuient aussi sur les données de la psychologie expérimentale, affective, sociale, etc. . . . .

La psychologie de Piaget étant prise comme cadre de référence, le concept opératoire comme le concept d'équilibration pourraient aussi s'appliquer à d'autres psychologies.

Les recherches en psychologie pédagogique étudient les problèmes d'apprentissage pour analyser plus finement les sources des difficultés d'assimilation, pour trouver des solutions et les proposer à une expérimentation pédagogique. Le psychologue participe à cette expérimentation. Les informations recueillies sur le plan de l'application permettent de réajuster la problématique posée pour les recherches d'apprentissage.

Le centre ou le laboratoire de psychologie pédagogique fonctionne avec la participation de l'Ecole.

b) La participation de l'Ecole sera une des premières difficultés à résoudre. La difficulté ne pourra être surmontée que grâce à une bienveillante compréhension des autorités scolaires. C'est une mentalité différente, une conception plus fondamentale de la pédagogie qu'il faudrait adopter. La pratique d'une expérimentation pédagogique demande plus de temps qu'une expérimentation dans un autre domaine.

La seconde difficulté réside dans la formation des maîtres. Sans une bonne formation en psychologie générale, sans les connaissances requises pour comprendre la psychologie génétique, sans la pratique des méthodes que la psychologie génétique a adoptées, la psychologie piagétienne, croyons-nous, ne sera que superficiellement comprise, par conséquent mal interprétée, ce qui en faussera l'application.

Pourquoi doit-on accorder encore plus d'importance que de coutume à la formation des maîtres lorsqu'on désire appliquer la psychologie de Piaget?

Le maître doit comprendre l'enfant. L'avertissement de J.J. Rousseau reste fondé "commencez par connaître vos élèves car, très assurément, vous ne les connaissez point". Cette connaissance ne doit pas se limiter à celle des lois du développement; c'est une connaissance de chaque enfant dont il s'agit, de chaque enfant qui agit dans un environnement donné — l'Ecole. L'enseignant est un psychologue qui à chaque instant, et pour chacun de ses élèves, confronte ses connaissances à la réalité pratique. Il adapte donc sa pédagogie en fonction de chacun de ses élèves en particulier.

Il doit avoir toujours présent à l'esprit le tableau "clinique" de chaque écolier. Toute intention de faire un apprentissage à l'enfant implique la connaissance préalable du niveau de son développement. De ce niveau dépendent la mobilisation des représentations imagées ou conceptuelles, l'adoption d'une certaine démarche dans la recherche de la solution d'un problème, la réponse à une question etc. — les références et les déductions auxquelles l'enfant doit recourir.

Cette complexité est saisie et ressentie par l'enseignant à propos de chaque élève et de chaque activité scolaire. La pédagogie devient ainsi une didactique clinique, clinique dans le sens que Piaget donne à sa méthode d'investigation essentiellement individuelle et casuistique.

Ce serait trop demander aux maîtres que d'exiger d'eux de telles compétences. Ce sont plutôt les responsables de la formation des maîtres qui doivent se convaincre de la nécessité d'une pédagogie clinique et, en conséquence, reviser le programme de la formation du corps enseignant.

Si la formation des maîtres est souvent confiée à une Faculté ou un Institut de niveau universitaire, ce n'est pas dans le simple but de revaloriser la fonction de l'enseignant, mais parce que l'enseignement universitaire s'appuie sur la recherche. On n'imagine pas un enseignement des sciences exactes qui ne se fonde pas sur la recherche; il serait, en effet, rapidement dépassé. De même, on ne peut imaginer un enseignement de la pratique pédagogique situé en dehors de la recherche, et sans lien avec elle.

Des centres ou des Instituts de recherche en psychologie pédagogique doivent travailler dans un esprit de coordination de la recherche fondamentale et de la recherche appliquée avec l'optique de fournir à la pratique pédagogique les données d'une nouvelle didactique.

Les recherches en psychologie génétique de Piaget nous ont fourni une base théorique. C'est à nous de savoir projeter ces modèles théoriques sur la réalité scolaire — en d'autres termes, rendre la solution opérationnelle pour l'Ecole. C'est à ce titre que l'on ne déformera pas la pensée de Piaget et que son oeuvre aura une influence déterminante sur les systèmes d'éducation.

VINH BANG

Assistant Director, Department of Psychology, School of Psychology and Education, University of Geneva

THE PSYCHOLOGY OF JEAN PIAGET AND ITS RELEVANCE TO EDUCATION

I have no desire to start a controversy, but I would like to begin by asking two questions: first, what has psychology contributed to education in general, and to the teaching-learning situation in particular; and second, what benefits has educational theory derived from psychology? If we were to assemble a group of psychologists and educators to discuss these two questions, the final answer would, I suspect, turn out to be, "Rather little."

The first to be surprised would probably be the psychologists, since the educators either have not known how, or have not been in a position to put psychology to use. Scientific psychology — whose growth, as everyone recognizes, has been rapid and varied — has fallen short of one of its goals, that of serving the individual and, consequently, of serving society.

If the psychologists become self-critical, then it is only fair that the educators take a close look at the schools. In my view, the prognosis will not be too hopeful, and a suitable therapy will have to be tried by psychologists and educators together.

I would like to describe a general framework for the contribution of psychology to educational theory, and within this framework to examine what currently is, and what might be, the influence of Piaget's work on the educational system.

Piaget has pointed out that all good psychology results in application. But application does not automatically come about. The orientation of a particular branch of psychology toward application does not imply that every psychologist must be a practitioner. It is the role of educational psychology in research to coordinate fundamental and applied research and to provide guidelines for applications.

Let me present a brief overview of the applications of psychology to educational theory. I know that it will upset some, and for that I apologize. Any far-reaching extrapolation is dangerous, but it does have the advantage of clarifying ideas and of emphasizing the essentials.

There are three branches of psychology that offer possibilities of application to education in general: psychometrics, child psychology, and affective psychology.

Psychometrics has devoted too much attention to research on diagnostic instruments. Its theoreticians consider empirical validation to be sufficient and accept as their basic data the results of education. Rather than investigate the causes of individual differences, they deal with the consequences of those differences.

Child psychologists have compiled increasingly elaborate descriptions of behavior and have brought to light certain essential characteristics. They have observed many interesting phenomena but they have been content with interpretation and have not proceeded to explanation.

Psychologists studying personality development have been able to serve education through therapeutic techniques, but in a limited way. Their success, though confined to a small number of individual cases, rests in the fact that they have looked for causes and not simply described conflicts and complexes. They have tried to return to the source, to the origins, in order to understand and, more particularly, to explain the various processes at work. Consistently, they have tried to go beyond observable phenomena.

The "remedial educator" must analyze the causes in order to understand the effects. He must investigate the formational process or the beginning of behavioral maladaptation in order to select the appropriate form of remedial education. Why should the educators not follow the same principles?

It is easy to criticize education, but we must also recognize the legitimacy of the criticisms leveled at psychometrics. Psychometrics has accentuated individual differences that have, in part, been created by the school, instead of developing an educational approach that would use individual differences constructively.

Child psychology has, I think, made our picture of the child more attractive. There is an analogy here with color television. It was thought that child psychology would offer a new dimension to the teacher. Instead, it has only added color to the picture he had before. Armed with child psychology, the teacher thinks that he understands his pupils, whereas he has only replaced a black and white picture with a colored one.

As for child psychotherapy, it is useful only for a very small number. In fact, it is possible that our educational system has helped to provide it with a clientele.

The application of psychology to education needs a complete reappraisal. The present crisis in education lends urgency to such a reexamination.

Up to now, psychology applied to education has tried to identify problem cases — that is, children who fail to adapt to the school situation — and to provide them with psychological aid, usually of a psychotherapeutic nature, so that they might be reintegrated into regular school activities. The question of whether the school is maladapted in relation to the natural development of the child is rarely asked.

Psychology accepts the school as it is, and the problem cases. It does a job of patching. It has seen its role reduced to that of a nursing service. Its responsibility is to help acute cases. However, psychology applied to education must be concerned with the normal pupil, the pupil who poses no immediate problem, although he also may encounter difficulties under conditions that require adaptation, or that are unfavorable to his development.

In my view, educational psychology should focus on prevention and, given this dimension, draw from science in general that which can assist the educator and, from child psychology, insights into the development of the child and the effects of education on him.

For the past fifteen years, educational psychology has tried to discover new approaches. Perhaps in the search for a contribution from psychology, perhaps in the critical assessment of this contribution, some educators have turned to the developmental psychology of Jean Piaget and the work of the Geneva School.

There are many who seek in the work of Piaget possible applications to the teaching-learning situation. This interest is due to the individual initiatives of researchers or of teachers who would like to introduce educational reforms in their classes or schools, and to more generalized programs such as the Nuffield Mathematics Project, which has been tried out in a group of elementary schools for five years. In this project, a whole new program and a new method of application have been elaborated, based on Piaget's research on the development of numerical, spatial, and geometric concepts in the child.

From these attempts at application, some observations can be made. As always happens in transposing from theory to practice, the application of the psychology of Piaget to education runs into difficulties. First, we must make a distinction between the interests of Piaget as he studies the child, and those of the educational psychologist who would like to contribute directly toward changes in the teaching-learning situation. Second, we must be aware of the need for intermediate research, between theoretical and applied research, to define the modes and conditions of educational experimentation based on Piagetian studies.

Piaget has invented a methodology to study the formation of concepts, and eventually to produce a theory of knowledge. The object of his study is the child, with a focus on the child's mental development. The importance of Piaget to the science of psychology is that he has tried to explain the development of cognitive structures.

Piaget began by studying the logic of the child and the development of logical structures with a view to understanding the acquisition of knowledge. He believed that this process could best be understood through a study of what children say.*

It was later, in 1947, that Piaget announced that he had adopted a new research methodology: "Instead of first analyzing the symbolic operations of thought, we will begin with the effective and concrete operations implied in action itself."** It was a new approach that led to an understanding of the reflective and reasoning processes of the child. In this methodology, the child manipulates certain simple materials and is asked to predict the outcomes of certain transformations, and also to explain why a particular outcome is possible.

Despite their difficulty in following the language of Piaget, many people have been influenced by his simple micro-experiential approach. One experiment, for example, consists of taking two identical glasses, pouring the same quantity of water into each, then repouring the contents of one of them into a third, wider glass, and asking a five-year-old child whether there is still the same amount of water in the criterion glass as in the wider glass.

Piaget's research constitutes a network of interlocking experiments: the result of one of them is the answer to one particular question and the point of departure for asking another. But the whole network of research is oriented toward one goal, namely, to try to explain cognitive development.

It was as a result of hundreds of pieces of research

* J. Piaget *Etudes sur la logique de l'enfant: Le langage et la pensée chez l'enfant.* Neuchâtel et Paris, Delachaux et Niestlé, 1923.

** J. Piaget Preface to the third edition of *Le jugement et le raisonnement chez l'enfant.* Neuchâtel et Paris, Delachaux et Niestlé, 1947.

undertaken with thousands of children that Piaget finally came to describe and explain the evolution and development of the "knowing subject", that is, if I may be permitted the expression, the child in general. This "knowing subject" is neither one particular child, nor the sum of all the children studied. Rather, it is *the* child. The school, on the other hand, must be concerned with each individual pupil.

Piaget has his own research goals, but educational psychology must define goals for itself. Some educational psychologists are actually utilizing Piaget's psychological insights as educational instruments. Unfortunately, they frequently misinterpret Piaget. For example, any researcher can replicate one of the Piagetian tasks and obtain the same results. However, if he does no more than that, he shows clearly that he has not really understood Piaget.

The wealth of observations — from the reflex actions of the new-born baby, to the reasoning processes of the adolescent and the propositional logic of formal adult thought — at first glance gives the impression that Piaget is easy to understand. The researcher who obtains the same results under the same observational conditions is led to believe that he has understood Piaget's theory. As a result, some well-intentioned psychologists and educators think that they can apply the results of Piaget's psychology to education simply by transforming the research techniques (for example, on the development of number concepts, of geometry, of space, of time, etc.) into exercises for students. Such a procedure is certainly doomed to failure. Teachers can thus quite justifiably consider Piaget's work questionable or, if they maintain a measure of confidence in him, they may reproach him for not being concerned about applied psychology and for not contributing to education.

We should not forget that educational psychology has its own interests and goals. "The child" is not its object of study. The developmental psychology of Piaget has made it possible to understand the child, but the role of education is to aid and guide the child in the acquisition of knowledge. A proper reconversion would consist of making the Piagetian model of child development operational for education in general and for the teaching-learning situation in particular.

The techniques used to study thought processes cannot simply be adopted as techniques for the teaching-learning situation. The research techniques, the material used for these investigations, are designed for a specific purpose. In the case of the transformation of a ball of plasticine into a sausage or a cake, or the pouring of a quantity of liquid into a glass that is wider or narrower than the criterion — the purpose is to produce conflict, between perceptual indices and the child's reasoning, a conflict that can be resolved through the logic of reciprocal compensations. The results of such experiments have led Piaget to construct a model of equilibration — "conservation" — that describes and explains one stage in the long process of mental development.

The teacher must be aware of the existence of such stages of mental development, for the child can deal correctly with physical invariants only if he has acquired "conservation". However, educators do not have to follow the same observational techniques to determine whether or not a child possesses the concept of conservation. Instead, they must ask themselves whether the existence of this concept has implications for their educational technique. For each level of development, educators must be aware of the existence of underlying structures. But because they have not understood this, some think that they should develop a systematic program to teach conservation as if it were an item in a grammar or arithmetic curriculum.

Some large publishing houses have tried to reproduce the research techniques for elementary logic, classification, and seriation in the form of practical exercises for the learning of mathematical logic. They have also introduced certain variations to "enrich" the material. While their intentions may have been good, they have unwittingly done more harm than good to Piaget. Their attempt is bound to fail sooner or later, for it is clear that these editors have not grasped in depth the ideas of developmental psychology. They have not understood that the micro-experiential approach of Piaget is not an end in itself. As a result, there is a risk that failures will be imputed to the theory, for which it is not responsible but which are due to the improper applications of the theory.

Let me try to show how educational psychology should take the psychology of Piaget into consideration. Although the scope of this paper is limited, I shall make some educational reflections on three concepts: the activity of the subject, the stages of development, and the clinical method.

The activity of the subject

It is through his own activity that the child constructs his intelligence. The activity of the infant is essentially sensorimotor. To this initial activity is added a representational activity in the period of the formation of the semiotic function. From that point, concrete activity serves as a support for mental activity. The subject's manipulations of real objects become a way of asking questions and of solving problems. In the period of concrete operations, the child is increasingly capable of predicting the outcomes of his manipulations. Finally, activity becomes essentially mental when the adolescent performs combinatorial operations on propositional data. It is not possible to understand the role of activity in the subject simply by observing his behavior, and it is the subject's mental activity that is of interest to the educational practitioner. External, observable activity can be understood only when one can explain the underlying intellectual activity (the operational grouping, in Piaget's terms).

Fifty years ago, the "activity school", like the "new education", had a poor understanding of the notion of "activity" in the pupil. To think is to perform operations, in the sense of mental processes. At one point in the child's development, this process is possible only if the child manipulates objects; and the child is active because he performs operations. To assign a school exercise is, in fact, to assign an activity that is rational, reflective, and creative. Every activity must be integrated into the network of activities that contributes to mental development. The way to establish such networks can be indicated by psychological studies of learning. It is in this direction that the Geneva School has for several years undertaken research into the acquisition of cognitive structures, the results of which will have a direct effect on education.

The stages of development

The results of some parallel research, conducted in different psychological laboratories, do not necessarily agree with the research done at Geneva on the correspondence between ages and stages.

According to Piaget, the three necessary conditions of a system of stages are that they follow one another in a constant order in all subjects; that each stage can be characterized by a general structure and not just by one predominant characteristic; and that the successive structures be integrated one into the next according to the order of their formation.

It is essential that educational psychologists recognize the idea of a universal, constant order of succession, with indispensable periods in which new intellectual structures are in the course of being established, and with stages of equilibrium. The term "stage" in the language of Piaget describes two different situations. First, there are the major stages of development: the period of sensorimotor intelligence, the period of concrete operations, and the period of formal operations; second, there are the stages in the construction of a particular concept, for example, the stages in the construction of the number concept.

The second idea that educational practice must recognize is the notion of a general structural network. The construction of number does not take place independently of the construction of geometry, or of the concepts of probability, causality, etc. The common denominator in this interdependence is the structure of an underlying operational grouping. We should note that educational theory has traditionally divided knowledge into disciplines: the teaching of language has been divided into grammar, vocabulary, pronunciation, reading, composition, diction, etc. A partial reform — similar to the one in the teaching of mathematics — should be encouraged, but such a reform, if it is not coordinated with other reforms, is vulnerable to the mistake made by associationism, in upholding the idea of an association of isolated mental activities. For this reason, research into applications should be undertaken within a broad framework.

The clinical method

Although this third point is not one of the concepts in the theory of psychogenetic development, but rather a research methodology adopted by Piaget for investigating the child's reasoning processes, I include it here because I want to describe a clinical approach to education.

This approach recognizes individual differences, not within the framework of psychometrics, which is interested in performance, but within the framework of an educational methodology that is adapted to the processes of the pupils' thought in assimilating a concept. The fact that different individuals perform in the same way does not necessarily mean that they employ the same representations, or that they operate on reality in the same way, or that they adopt the same strategies for finding a solution. It is through the study of these individual differences that we can understand creativity, an important area of research in education.

A clinical approach to education thus goes beyond a didactic approach based on Piaget's theory because it combines the understanding of the development of "the child" with an awareness of individual differences.

Several conditions are necessary if the developmental

psychology of Piaget is to have an effect on any given educational approach. In my view, the first step is to make the insights of Piagetian psychology operational in the field of education. This step can only be taken through the establishment of a body of intermediate research which, for the purpose of this discussion, we shall call research in educational psychology. This research is not based solely on the theory of Piaget, but depends also on the contributions of experimental psychology, affective psychology, social psychology, and other branches.

Taking Piaget's psychology as a frame of reference, the concept of mental operations, like the equilibration concept, can also be applied to other psychological approaches.

Research studies in educational psychology are concerned with learning in order to analyze more closely the sources of difficulty in assimilation, in order to find solutions and to submit them for educational evaluation. Psychologists participate in this evaluation. Information gathered at the level of application permits the reformulation of problems for research in learning.

The center or the laboratory for research in educational psychology must function with the participation of the school, and that participation is one of the first problems that must be solved. This difficulty can only be overcome through acceptance and understanding on the part of school officials. They must acquire a different point of view, a more fundamental concept of education. Educational experimentation requires more time than experimentation in other areas.

The education of teachers raises another problem. If they have not received a good education in general psychology, and if they have not received introductory background and practical experience in the methodology of developmental psychology, they will acquire only a superficial understanding of Piagetian psychology. They will interpret it badly and apply it wrongly.

Why is it necessary to pay more attention than usual to teacher education when one wishes to apply the psychology of Piaget? The teacher must understand the child. There is a saying of Rousseau: "Begin by getting to know your students, for certainly you do not know them." The teacher's knowledge should not be restricted to the laws of cognitive development but should encompass the understanding of each child who acts in a given environment, the school. The teacher is a psychologist who at each instant, and for each of his pupils, has to test his understanding against practical reality. Thus, he adapts his educational methodology to each of his pupils.

The teacher must always have in mind the "clinical chart" of each pupil. Every intention to teach the child implies a preliminary knowledge of his level of development. On this developmental level depends the child's ability to utilize mental images or conceptual representations — to adopt a particular strategy in the search for a solution to a problem, or to choose the data he has to take into account and the deductions he has to make.

If this complex of abilities is perceived and understood by the teacher for each student and for each school activity, educational methodology can become a clinical methodology, clinical in the sense that Piaget's investigatory method deals with individuals and with causes.

It is too much to expect teachers spontaneously to feel the need for this competence. Rather, it is those who are responsible for teacher education who must be convinced of the necessity for a clinical approach to education, and who must revise the programs of teacher education.

If teacher education is often entrusted to faculties or institutes at the university level, it is not simply to improve the status of the profession, but because teaching at the university level is combined with research. It is impossible to conceive of teaching the exact sciences without basing that teaching on research. The teaching would very soon be out of date. Likewise, it is impossible to conceive of teaching educational methods without basing the teaching on research.

The centres and institutes for research in educational

psychology must try to coordinate basic research and applied research with a view to providing, to the educational practitioner, insights for a new educational methodology.

The research of Piaget in developmental psychology has provided a theoretical foundation. It is left to us to project his theoretical models onto the reality of the schools; in other words, to make the solutions operational for the schools. In this way, the thought of Piaget will remain intact, yet his work will have a determining influence on the educational system.

(Translation by Bruce Rusk)

PATRICK SUPPES

Director, Institute for Mathematical Studies in the Social Sciences, Stanford University

ALTERNATIVES THROUGH COMPUTERS

To provide some historical perspective on the anticipated role that computers will play in our society, I would like briefly to review what I consider to be the three great educational technologies that have preceded the introduction of computers.

The first was the founding of libraries in the ancient world, the most important example being the famous Alexandrian Library that was established about 300 B.C. Because of the seductive charms of Plato and the Greek dramatists, it is easy to forget that the real intellectual center of the Hellenistic world, from a broader standpoint, was Alexandria and not Athens. From about 250 B.C. to A.D. 400, not only was Alexandria the most important center of mathematics and astronomy in the ancient world, but it was also a major center of literature, especially because of the collection in the Alexandrian Library. The first real beginnings of critical scholarship in the western world in literature, the editing of texts, the analysis of style, the drawing up of bibliographies were achieved in the Alexandrian Library. I see as the first technological revolution in education the organization of large bodies of learning in a given place. Libraries of a substantial nature were to be found in major cities of the ancient world, not to mention the collections of learning in China and other civilizations. The recognition that learning needed to be collected in a single place, and in a written form that would provide continuity and a basis for continued intellectual activity of a higher order, was the first major revolution. The technological part of this revolution was the organization of libraries like that at Alexandria.

The second major technological revolution was the introduction of printing. The historic date in the West, as we all learned early in school, was 1452, for the printing of the Gutenberg Bible. Block printing on a substantial scale began several centuries earlier in China and Korea. In the western world, the introduction of printing meant that men of affluence could have substantial libraries of their own in the sixteenth century, and the records show a great outpouring of printing of learned works in that century. It is sometimes mistakenly thought that a widespread printing of books began at the same time for student use in schools. This was not the case. The method of recitation that dominated the Middle Ages continued not only in the sixteenth and seventeenth centuries, but well into the eighteenth century. In fact, the use of recitation to teach some subjects, such as elementary arithmetic, continued far into the nineteenth century. The widespread use of books in schools did not occur until the latter part of the eighteenth century, at the earliest.

This brings me to the third technological revolution, the introduction of mass education through schools. When we think about schools, we tend to think about them in a very limited way. We think of them as having been here forever and as staying forever, and we think that they are going to sustain about the same form that we have experienced ourselves. But even for North America, this reverie is false as to the facts. The first national statistics on education of a systematic sort were begun in the United States by the U.S. Office of Education in 1870, and for that year, it was estimated that just 57 per cent of the young people between five and seventeen years of age were in school. Of the seventeen-year-old group, only 2 per cent were graduates from high school. Public schools that involve the bulk of the population are strictly a phenomenon of the twentieth century. For most of the world, they are not even a phenomenon of the twentieth century, but are of much more recent creation. In tropical Africa, until the last decade, a negligible percentage of the students went on to secondary school, and in some countries only 10 or 15 per cent completed elementary school. Similar data obtain for developing countries in other parts of the world.

Given that the phenomenon of schools is so recent and yet plays such an important part in our society, it is not difficult to turn to computers to provide the opportunity for a fourth major technological revolution in education. I want to explore some of the alternatives to schools that are offered by computers. The purpose of my preliminary remarks is to emphasize how transient the phenomenon of mass education has been and, consequently, how relatively easy it would be to change it. Schools are not institutions that are deeply embedded in the culture of western civilization, or in the civilization of any other part of the world. Their shape and form have been constantly subject to change. There is no reason that schools must exist as they have for the past thirty or forty years. It might be thought that universities offer a more continuous and constant history, but this is true only for the select institutions. Higher education for the bulk of the population is of course an even more recent phenomenon than mass education at the elementary and secondary levels. We have just begun to explore the alternatives to the traditional university organization. I shall consider several possibilities in this paper.

Computers as instructional devices

Before considering some of the alternative organizational structures computers make possible, it will perhaps be useful to examine briefly the way in which computers can be used as instructional devices. Current applications of computers in our society range from the automatic control of factories to data-bank searches for credit ratings. A high percentage of regular employees in Canada and the United States is paid by computerized payroll systems. Increasingly, in a variety of biological and physical experimentation in the sciences, computers are used for on-line monitoring and control of experiments. The use of computers for administrative purposes, such as that of payroll, is familiar now to most people. The way in which computers can be used for instruction, however, is not yet widely known and it may be useful to review, even if briefly, the operating procedures.

In the first place, because of the computer's great speed, it can handle simultaneously a large number of students. Each student can be working at a different point in a particular curriculum, or be in a completely different curriculum. In the simplest mode of operation, the student sits at a terminal device that is something like an electric typewriter or a teletype. Messages are typed out by the computer, and the student in turn can enter his responses on the keyboard. To augment this simple typewriter terminal, perhaps the most important next feature is to add an audio capacity to deliver messages under computer control. The next step in complexity is to add graphic and pictorial displays as, for example, to a television terminal under computer control. In our own work at Stanford, because of the relatively low cost, we mainly use teletype terminals. In the world of the future, more complex terminal configurations of the kind I have described will be widely available.

Some of you may be saying, "So what? So a computer can operate quickly and therefore handle a number of students; a good lecturer can talk to a lot of students also. What's so unusual about what a computer can do?" I think the central argument for instruction by computer may be found in an examination of the deep possibilities of *individualized* instruction. The first and most important aspect of individualization is based on the well-known psychological generalization that there are definite and clearly significant individual differences in students. The fact is that children enter school with remarkably different abilities and retain them throughout their careers; further, they work at different rates and at different levels of accuracy and understanding. But, unfortunately, for obvious economic reasons, schools and colleges are not able to offer an individual curriculum program to each student according to his needs. The computer, simultaneously handling many students, can let each progress at his own pace and at his own level of achievement.

A different and equally important aspect of individualization is the immediate correction of individual student responses when an error is made. It is an instructive experience to compare first-graders in class with first-graders at computer terminals, to observe the effects of giving the student immediate correction and reinforcement for his responses. I expect that the same stimulus would be observed in the teaching of elementary skills at the university level. Our computer-based Russian course at Stanford demands the attention of the student during the entire fifty-minute period, because his part of the program is solely concerned with his own responses and his own work. No such individual attention can possibly be given in the classroom. In a class of ten or fifteen, the student knows that when he gives a response, almost certainly the teacher will call upon another student, not himself, for the next response. He can immediately relax and let his mental machinery idle for the next few minutes. With a computer terminal, the situation is more like that of having an individual tutor.

Let me turn now to various possible levels of interaction between the student and the computer program. Following a current usage, I shall refer to each of the instructional programs as a particular system of instruction. At the simplest level, *individualized drill-and-practice systems* are meant to supplement the regular curriculum taught by the teacher. The introduction of concepts and new ideas is handled in conventional fashion by the teacher. The role of the computer is to provide regular review and practice in basic concepts and skills. In the case of elementary mathematics, for example, each student receives daily a certain number of exercises that are automatically presented, evaluated and scored by the computer program without any effort by the classroom teacher. Moreover, these exercises can be presented on an individualized basis, with the brighter students receiving exercises that are harder than average, and the slower ones receiving problems that are easier than average.

One important aspect of this kind of individualization should be emphasized. It is not necessary to decide at the beginning of the school year in which track a student should be placed; for example, he need not be classified as a slow student for the entire year. Individualized drill-and-practice work is suitable to all the elementary subjects that occupy a good part of the curriculum. Elementary mathematics, elementary science, and the initial work in a foreign language are typical parts of the curriculum that benefit from standardized and regularly presented drill-and-practice exercises. A large computer with 200 terminals can handle as many as 6,000 students on a daily basis in this instructional mode. In all likelihood, it will soon be feasible to increase these numbers to 1,000 terminals and 30,000 students.

At the second and deeper level of interaction between student and computer program, *tutorial systems* take over the main responsibility both for presenting a concept and for developing the skills necessary for its use. The intention is to approximate the interaction a patient tutor would have with an individual student. An important aspect of the reading and elementary mathematics tutorial programs, with which we have been concerned at Stanford in the past ten years, is that every effort is made to avoid an initial experience of failure on the part of the slower children. On the other hand, the program has enough flexibility to avoid boring the brighter children with endlessly repetitive exercises. As soon as the student manifests a clear understanding of a concept, on the basis of handling a number of exercises, he is moved on to a new concept and new exercises.

At the third and deepest level of interaction, *dialogue systems* are aimed at permitting the student to conduct a genuine dialogue with the computer. The dialogue systems at present exist primarily at the conceptual rather than the operational level, and I do want to emphasize that in the case of dialogue systems a number of difficult technical problems must first be solved. One problem is that of recognizing spoken speech. Especially in the case of young children, we should like the child simply to be able to ask the computer program a question. To permit this interaction, we must be able to recognize the spoken speech of the child and also to recognize the meaning of the question he is asking. The problem of recognizing meaning is at least as difficult as that of recognizing the spoken speech. It will be some time before we shall be able to do either of these things with any efficiency and economy.

I would predict that within the next decade many children will use individualized drill-and-practice systems in elementary school; by the time they reach high school, tutorial systems will be available on a broad basis. Their children may in turn use dialogue systems throughout their school experience.

If these predictions are even approximately correct, they have far-reaching implications for education and society. Let me now turn to some of these implications.

Alternative educational structures

Let me give one or two examples of changes we can effect in the structure of educational institutions by using appropriately the new technology of computers and television. Because of my own special interest in computers, I shall concentrate on computer possibilities; but it should be understood that television would also be a component for the proposed changes in structure.

My first example concerns the organization of high

schools. An American phenomenon much discussed in the history of education in the twentieth century has been the introduction of the consolidated high school that brings together students from small schools to a centrally located large school that offers a variety of educational opportunities and resources to the students. The American consolidated high school is one of the glories of the history of education. Today, however, many of us feel that the large high school has become one of the most difficult institutions to deal with from a social standpoint. The mass aggregation of adolescents in one spot creates an environment that is on the one hand impersonal, and on the other potentially frictional and explosive, partly because of the large numbers of students and supervising adults in close quarters.

The use of our new technology will make possible an alternative structure that will return us to the small schools of the past. The ideal high school of the future may consist of no more than a hundred students and, in many cases, be located close to students' homes; or it may be a specialized school, catering to students' particular interests. The variety of curriculum and other educational resources, such as libraries, that has been so important a feature of the consolidated high school, will be made available by computer and television technology. I should say in this connection that the changes that can be brought about through the use of computers are more drastic and more radical than those that can be effected only through television. The difference is the possibility of a high level of interaction between the computer program and the student, the sort of thing that is not possible with a standard television lecture or laboratory demonstration.

In connection with the development of small schools, I believe that the introduction of computers as instructional devices is just as inevitable as the introduction of books in the past, even though there could be resistance from educational liberals. It is easy to imagine a refrain that could have been heard in the eighteenth century, to the effect that it is terrible to create an impersonal distance between the teacher and the student by handing the student a book and not letting him listen to the lilting voice of the teacher's same kinds of arguments about impersonal- niliar and have the same superficiality. As I ɔ emphasize in the preceding discussion, the . can provide more individualization and more ᴜual attention for the student, not less, than the ᴜeacher in those parts of instruction — like the teaching of basic skills — that require a high level of active response from the student.

I want to emphasize, however, that I do not see the computer as an instructional device in competition with the teacher. The role of the computer is like the role of books: to amplify the skills and time of the teacher. The economics of education will not, in any immediate future, change so as to reduce the student-teacher ratio at any level of education in any part of the world. Skilled teachers, however, will be able to use computers to individualize instruction in the standard parts of the curriculum and to reserve their own efforts for troubleshooting and individual attention of an intensive sort.

Because many of you will not be familiar with the rich possibilities that may be embedded in computer programs for instruction, it is important to emphasize the many ways a computer program can do things that a tutor cannot. For example, a computer program can prepare individualized student lessons from a large data base in a fashion that would be realistically impossible for a tutor, and certainly impossible for a teacher handling ten, twenty, or thirty students.

My second major example concerns alternatives to elementary schools. Through most of the history of civilization, young children have been taught primarily at home, often perhaps in an extended family group. We now have the technical possibility of returning the student to the home or to small neighborhood groups. Although these alternatives have not yet been thoroughly explored, it is important that discussion of their availability begin as early as possible. As far as I know, the new romantics in education have not discussed the radical possibility of dissolving elementary schools entirely and returning the child to the home — or to neighborhood groups of three or four homes — for his education.

In describing this possibility, let me emphasize that I am not maintaining that it is necessarily a wise move. I do, however, think it important that this technical possibility is now available. At the very least, it should be explored experimentally. By proper use of computer technology, the basic skills of reading, mathematics, and language arts can easily be brought to the student in the home or in a cluster of homes. Parts of the elementary science curriculum also can be handled by computer. Other parts of the elementary science curriculum, of the social studies program, and much of the work in art and music could be handled by television. I envisage a situation in which a master teacher would divide his time among several units. The mothers of the children would assume responsibilities for supervision and some would work as teachers' aides. This would be completely natural, because of the proximity of the school to their homes. In many urban settings, for example, it would be natural to place classrooms in apartment complexes. In other districts, a small one-room building could be added, or it might even be feasible to pay a small rent to one of the families for the use of space in a home. The main thing to avoid is heavy capital expenditure for physical plants; we have had too much of it in the past.

The third alternative structure deals with higher education. Here the possibilities are perhaps the easiest to implement and may be realized sooner than the others. In the areas surrounding Stanford, several community colleges are already offering courses for credit by television. As we face the costs throughout the world of providing higher education for increasing numbers, the use of computers and television to reduce costs and to decentralize the educational effort seems almost inevitable. One can see terminals available in apartment complexes for students at the community college level. At a later stage, one can envisage terminals in plants where employees work full-time, but also actively pursue their education. I should mention that in California, for example, a reasonable percentage of students in the state higher educational system are employed full-time, simultaneously with their enrollment as students. The development of such a delivery system for higher education will also naturally answer demands for continuing education for adults. At a more distant date, one can expect the terminal resources described earlier to be available in the home for the teaching of a wide range of subjects, from foreign languages to advanced technical courses in science and mathematics.

It may seem expensive to introduce such a delivery system for higher education. However, elementary computations show that if we replace the capital costs of campuses with expenditures for setting up the delivery system, the costs become competitive with the current costs of higher education. I shall not go into detailed calculations, but it is possible to back up this statement with a quantitative analysis.

Outstanding problems

My natural state of mind is skeptical and empirical. I am not inclined to make over-optimistic predictions about alternative structures in education in the immediate future. I do, however, think that the predictions I have sketched will be part of the future in a time scale that is not yet easy to forecast. I would like to conclude by discussing some of the major problems that stand in the way of a more rapid development of such alternative structures.

Economic problems. Computers are expensive, and it is difficult to organize a delivery system, as described, at an acceptable cost. There are a couple of points worth emphasizing. As a large number of students are placed on a given computer system, the cost of the central computer is less important than the cost of individual terminals and telephone communications. This is true, certainly, for a system that has on the order of 1,000 terminals and handles between 20,000 and 30,000 students a day. Part of the problem is the large initial capital investment. Another part of the economic problem is the operating cost. Perhaps the most important economic problem, however, is to be tough-minded about ways in which technology can actually substitute for labor-intensive efforts by teachers. These problems have just begun to be explored. A great tradition in education is that every new technology simply becomes an add-on cost to the present bill for instruction. In the future, it will likely be impossible to sustain this system. The economics of education will demand that technology be used as a substitute for rather than as a supplement to teachers. This is not a problem for teachers, in my judgement. It means that the skills required of teachers will increase, the professional requirements for teachers will increase, their status and compensation will correspondingly increase, but the absolute number of teachers relative to a given population of students will decrease.

Institutional problems. Problems of institutional change are poorly understood. There is evidence that universities, for example, are among the most conservative institutions in our society. In any case, the rapid development of alternative structures for education will be neither simple nor easy. On the other hand, the willingness of community colleges, which do not have a long tradition, to consider new methods of instruction and new approaches is encouraging. There are problems of prejudice and entrenchment, but there are also intellectual problems of understanding the kinds of organization we want for the future. The technology affords many possibilities, but we have not thought through which of these possibilities we consider the most advantageous, the most interesting, or the most exciting.

The central idea I have been stressing is that through

computers we have the means to develop alternative structures that will effectively decentralize the present educational system. The issue of decentralization of services, of places of work, of almost all aspects of our life is gradually coming to the fore as a central social and political problem of the last part of the twentieth century. The issues involved in decentralizing education will be among the most significant of these problems of decentralization. The problems that face us are not really technological: they are conceptual, institutional, and social. I have certainly not made any concrete suggestions for tackling these problems; at most, I wished to bring them to your attention.

Intellectual problems. Finally, there are intellectual and scientific problems that surround a proposed deepening of the use of technology. We are on the edges of some major problems that need to be solved. As yet, we have a fairly simple-minded set of explicit ideas as to making computer programs conduct sophisticated dialogues with students and be perceptive of students' needs. The difficulty is not technological, but scientific. We do not have an explicit understanding of the way in which one intelligent human being conducts a meaningful conversation with another. It is a limitation that is as old as Plato. Many of us can talk well, and sometimes even listen, but we have a poor understanding of how we do it. We have no analytical grasp of the structure of a dialogue. We do not know what the ingredients of intellectual discourse are between tutor and student, and until we have this deeper understanding we shall not be able to reach as far as we want with the kinds of technology discussed.

Aristotle said that man is a rational animal. I would prefer to say that man is a talking animal. A curious, interesting, and deeply human fact about man's technology is this: a deeper and subtler intellectual command of, say, computer technology is completely coupled with a central area of research on human beings themselves. The understanding of how we use language, the understanding of the structure of our language, and the understanding of why we say what we do when we do, are all involved. As we acquire such understanding of ourselves, we can apply it to education in deep and powerful ways with the aid of technology.

NORTHROP FRYE

University Professor, University of Toronto

THE DEFINITION OF A UNIVERSITY

In a recent interview I was asked why I wanted to present a definition of the university to an audience that might not be profoundly interested in the subject. I suggested that there were two reasons. First, the superstitions and the pseudo-concepts of educational methodology have not made much impact on the university, at least so far, and consequently the university can still serve as a model of educational aims. The second and more important reason, I said, is that, being a voluntary enterprise, at least technically, the university does not have the penal quality that universal compulsory education necessarily acquires. The word "penal" slipped out without my intending it, and I wondered afterwards why I had used a word that might possibly be offensive.

As I began to think about this, certain visions of my own childhood days arose in my mind. I saw children lined up and marched into a grimy brick building at nine in the morning, while a truant officer prowled the streets outside. The boys and girls were sent in through sexually separated entrances: it was regarded as a matter of the highest importance that a boy should not go through a door marked "girls" even if no act of excretion was involved. They then

filed into their classrooms, found their desks and sat down
with their hands folded in front of them in what was
referred to as "sitting position". At that point a rabble of
screaming and strapping spinsters was turned loose on
them, and the educational process began. The deterrent to
idleness in this setup was being kept in, or having one's
sentence lengthened. As the students grew older, the atmosphere of the classroom came to resemble that of an armed
truce. There was a high correlation between a boy's ability
to disturb a classroom and his popularity with his class-
mates, as he himself well knew. The boys, for the most
part, resisted the educational process openly, their resistance being either sullen or boisterous, depending on tem-
perament. The girls, on the other hand, were far more
docile; they tended to be obedient and to do as they were
told. It was many years before I realized that docility was
by far the more effective form of resistance.

I remember a good deal of unconscious sadism on both
sides — teachers as well as students. But there was not, of
course, the built-in brutality that goes with teaching the
younger members of a ruling class, and that belongs to
expensive and exclusive public schools. I remember that I
had a good deal of sympathy and some liking for my
teachers, but I think only one of them was an influence on
me. That was my music teacher, with whom I had a purely
voluntary and extracurricular connection. He had no truant
officer behind him, but he did have the only authority that
matters — the authority that springs from a genuine knowledge and love of his subject. The last time I went to see
him, he was still dwelling on what had been obviously one
of the happiest evenings of his life, an evening during the
war when two desperately lonely British airmen, stationed
at a camp near by, had phoned and said, "We hear you're a
musician. Is it all right if we come up just to talk about
music?"

Now you will say that this picture is a very different one
from what you remember, to say nothing of what those of
you who are teachers would want to produce in your own

classrooms. There has been a good deal of change. There should have been, in forty years. I will come to the reasons for some of the change later. But there has been a good deal of continuity too.

I find that I think very little about my school days, but that I think much more about the kind of society that lay behind the school and the kind of assumptions it had built into it, conscious and unconscious. For example, one of the things that bored me to death with public schools was the fact that our textbooks were so grotesquely out of date. In the twenties of this century, our geography book talked of Germany's "newly acquired province of Alsace-Lorraine", and the maps were of the same vintage. The British history was written by someone who was not quite certain of the outcome of the Boer War. The physiology book explained with diagrams how women distorted their viscera by tight lacing, and the physics book talked glibly about ether. This was, I recognize, a purely local flowering of incompetence, and it would not have had its direct counterpart elsewhere. Nevertheless, it comes close to the two permanent defects in education. One is the pathetic illusion that new methods of teaching can make up for an out-of-date conception of the subject, or for a steadily increasing ignorance of the subject. Publishers understand this illusion very well, and they continually push new gimmicks because they realize that a genuinely new conception of a subject would cause immediate panic. This is why every week I get brochures for textbooks on literary criticism based on conceptions of literary theory that would have been antiquated to Samuel Johnson and primeval to Coleridge.

The other assumption that allowed such textbooks to exist was, I think, even more important. It was a feeling that children ought to be kept off the streets not only physically but mentally. This assumption is related to that curious conception of the limbo of "adolescence" — the conception that there ought to be a period of life, between puberty and voting age, in which young people should be, to some extent, segregated from what is going on in the world. This conception of the adolescent can hardly have any basis in biology: it is a deliberate creation of industrial society, and one wonders why such a creation was made. A frequent explanation, advanced by Robert Hutchins, is that the reason is economic. The attempt is to slow down productivity or, as Hutchins says, to turn American education into a gigantic playpen in order to keep young people off the labor market. I think this is quite possibly a part of the explanation, but by no means the whole of it. I want to return to this question; meanwhile, I should like to make it clear that when I use the word "adolescent" I do not refer primarily to young people, but to a social neurosis that has been projected on young people.

Some of the things that I learned at school were not what I was intended to learn. There was a barrage of propaganda directed against smoking and drinking, which, so far as I could gather, had no effect whatever on the mores of the community, a large portion of which drank its way all through prohibition with the greatest enthusiasm. I dare say that similar propaganda against drugs goes on in the schools now, even in communities where half the population is employed in pushing drugs at the other half. What I learned was that propaganda is entirely useless unless it can suggest some kind of participatory role for those at whom it is addressed. It is not because the propaganda was negative that it was ineffective. Negative propaganda can, unfortunately, sometimes be very effective. In Nazi Germany it was possible to convince German children that Jews were of a different human type from themselves, even though their senses and their reason were telling them the opposite. But propaganda based merely on the "don't do that" formula is clearly wasted effort.

The schools were also designed to teach what was referred to as good grammar, that is, a standard English that no one spoke or even tried to speak. I remember one remark of a teacher, "Tomorrow we will go on to the lesson on 'shall' and 'will', because I would like to finish it by Friday." The language of the recess ground was unaffected by the learned language, partly for class reasons: colloquial language was the reassuring speech of those who belonged; "good grammar" represented the unpopular minority cult of intellect and culture. I noted, also, two things that were rigidly excluded from all our reading material: the themes of sex and violence. I began to understand why sex and violence are the most genuinely popular elements of popular culture.

Why was there so little sense of participation? I think it was partly because of another unconscious assumption on the part of society, that Johnny should go to school because it was natural for him not to want to. That is, what he naturally wanted to do, according to this assumption, was play, but to be sent to school was to be enrolled in a civilizing operation. Civilization, then, was assumed to be antagonistic to nature. This assumption, that civilization takes the form of an authoritarian domination of nature, is exactly the same assumption that has produced, in other aspects of our society, the tedious grid pattern of our streets, our countrysides, and now even of our buildings. The same assumption is behind our pollution problems, behind the almost unimaginable hideousness of urban sprawl, behind the wanton destruction of trees and rivers and animals. There, if I had had eyes to see it, was the central paradox of the contemporary world. It was all around me at school, and it was still all around me after I went to college, enrolled in a course in philosophy, and settled down to grapple with some of its primary texts, including Aristotle's *Metaphysics,* the first sentence of which reads, "All men by nature desire to know."

It is customary when a class is ready to leave school or college to ask a convocation speaker to come and tell them that they have finished their education and are ready to go out into the world. I have a genuine sympathy with convocation speakers, because I have probably made as many such speeches in my time as anyone else in the country, but that is one theme that I have never used. It is obvious that nobody ever goes out into the world at all, and that when one is ready to leave school the social order simply picks him up and drops him into a different file. We leave school and we get a job, and the job is psychologically identical with the school as I have described it. The job is nearly always penal: it is endured so that one can enjoy one's spare time outside it without crippling anxiety, and perhaps with some hope of getting more spare time as one becomes more senior. But from biblical times there has been a tendency to regard work as partial reparation for what the soul in a poem of Yeats calls "the crime of birth".

The motive behind compulsory universal education was on the whole a benevolent one. The motive was that in a democracy one had to be trained to participate in a very complex society. At the age of six one may think that one does not want the training, but one will want it later. Education that seems to the child irrelevant is not really irrelevant so much as tentative. A girl in high school may feel that she can't do algebra because it does not correspond to the vision of the kind of life she thinks she wants to lead. But the community mildly compels her to try a little algebra, because this is a democracy and it is her right to be exposed to quadratic equations, however little she wants them. And still what all this benevolence has produced in society is a kind of maximum security prison, maximum because it is impossible to escape to the world outside. There is no world outside. There was once a convict at Alcatraz who got out of the prison library a book of poems, opened it and saw the two lines of a poem by Lovelace: "Stone walls do not a prison make, nor iron bars a cage." He looked around him and said, "Well, if that's true, this is one damn good imitation." Yet I think the poet was right as well as the inmate. A prison is any enclosure that gives claustrophobia to those who are inside it. We meet this sense of claustrophobia everywhere in society. So the question arises, "How did benevolence produce a prison?"

I begin my approach to this by distinguishing and contrasting two different kinds of habit or repetition. There is one kind of habit or repetition which is the basis of the whole learning process. It is the habit of practice, of progress through repeated, sometimes mechanically repeated, effort, which we see in anyone who is learning to play the piano or memorize the multiplication table. It is habit in the medieval sense of *habitus,* in which a man who could read Latin was said to have the habit of Latin; that is, he had practised Latin and had repeated the practice until he had it in his mind. There was a man in New York who lost his way in Manhattan, stopped an old lady and said, "How do I get to Carnegie Hall?" The old lady said, "Practice, practice." Practice in this sense is the basis of all mental activity and of all creative activity as well.

But there is another kind of habit or repetition that is exactly the opposite. This is the kind of anxiety-habit that is created by the fact that we change roles so frequently during the course of a day, often to the point of feeling that our identity is threatened. So we adopt ritual patterns of behavior, patterns of compulsive repetition, in order to establish a sense of continuous identity in our minds. This pattern of repetition — inorganic, clung to out of fear — is one that gradually moves us further and further from what we are in contact with. Thus the benevolence that produced the compulsory universal education bill became habitual and, because it was habitual, it became binding. Conditions change, and when attitudes toward those conditions do not change, into human life there comes a curious Hegelian fatality that eventually produces the opposite of what was originally aimed at. One could give many examples. A very simple one from current events would be the career of President Nixon, who was elected on a promise that he would try to unite the country, and who within two years has come to a position in which he can keep going only by trying to divide it. A different kind of example would be afforded by the relations of Canada and the United States. When the United States invaded Canada in 1812, it ran into a strong separatist sentiment and some well-organized guerrilla tactics, and the Americans failed to conquer Canada as ignominiously as they are now failing to conquer

North Vietnam. So they opted for peace and an undefended border, with the result that Canada is today almost the only country in the world that is a pure colony, a colony psychologically as well as economically. It now has the same relation to the United States that the United States had to Great Britain before 1776, except for the revolutionary sentiment. Even the institution under whose auspices this series of lectures has been offered is sometimes regarded — only by the uninformed, of course — as a cross between an occupying garrison and a colonial governor's mansion.

This phenomenon of things reversing themselves is particularly noticeable when society fastens on to something as a symbol for its anxiety and tries to maintain it without change. A good example would be the attitude to women in middle-class Victorian society. Women in that society were made the focus of the social anxieties of their time: they were supposed to be the keepers of good manners, of proper speech, and proper behavior. Hence the conditions set up for them subordinated them under the guise of protecting them. They could not vote and, if they were married, could not own property, because they were regarded as "pure", purity, like impurity, being a conception that always involves social segregation. The result of making women the custodians of Victorian anxieties was, of course, that that society became very largely matriarchal. Women accepted the ethos that had been handed them, and proceeded to impose it on the rest of society. I could give many examples from Victorian novels. One of the most incisive, perhaps, is in George Eliot's *Middlemarch*, which tells us how Dr. Lydgate, a brilliant scientist and a most original doctor, wanted a typically Victorian wife who would not disturb him intellectually and who would look decorative at his parties. So he married a beautiful, stupid, and insipid woman who promptly took his life over. In no time at all he lost all his originality and his eminence as a scientist and became simply a stuffed shirt giving the kinds of parties at which his wife could appear.

Around the time that I was going to school, society was beginning to create another focus of anxiety on the young. This was a feeling that young people ought to be left in an age of innocence before they got into the "rat race". Why should they get old before their time? Why should they take on responsibilities that they need not take on? Young people so fresh and attractive ought to be relieved from social responsibilities, and so symbolize the dream of leisure, of getting away from it all, that older people feel they have missed in life. And so there came a social system that both subordinated and protected young people, in the age group from puberty to majority, and did with adolescence substantially what the Victorian middle class had done to women. The result was the same: the growth and eventual domination of society by an adolescent ethos. This ethos now dominates the mass market, forcing women of sixty into miniskirts; it dominates entertainment; and now it tends increasingly to dominate politics, what with kidnapping, stone-throwing, rioting, and similarly adolescent forms of facing reality. Again, I repeat that my term adolescence refers to a social fixation that is represented by young people, but does not originate with them. The youthful activist who talks about his resentment against "authoritarianism" and "establishments" and "power structures" is falling into the anxiety role prescribed for him by his elders. Hence the paradox, which of course is not really a paradox at all, that the more he asserts his equality with those a generation older, the less of such equality he actually feels and the more typically "adolescent" his behavior becomes.

The "adolescent" is by definition immature, and the question of maturity, therefore, becomes a major social problem. About twenty years ago there was quite a cult of maturity, and people wrote books with titles like *The Mature Mind.* (I remember one such book written by a very famous psychologist, whose name you would recognize if I gave it, in which he said that the mature way to stop war was to learn to minimize the combative impulses. That is a strong contender for the title of the least informative sentence that I have ever read.) But the word maturity is out of fashion now. When, for example, a university administrator is faced by a student deputation demanding the instant and total reform of something, he is strongly tempted to use the word "immature" to describe their demands. He does not do so, partly because it would only make things worse, and partly because he realizes that they don't want the reform anyway, but have merely been told to demand it by an organizer with his mind on "higher" things. Nevertheless, if he did use the term, it seems to me that the students would have a right to say, immature in relation to what? If by maturity you mean either being resigned to or accepting conditions in our society that we regard as foolish and evil, we don't want your maturity; we would rather be immature. Whatever one thinks of that answer, one often has to ask oneself the complementary question in a time of crisis: "Where are the mature people?"

Last year I went through the People's Park crisis in Berkeley, California, which struck me as a preposterous, silly, and totally unnecessary event. It would have been easy to dismiss it as an immature and irresponsible action. But who was being mature? It wasn't the university teaching staff, which was demoralized. It wasn't the police, who were being given the most incredibly stupid orders. And it certainly was not the government of the state, which showed a considerable degree of low cunning in exploiting the situation, but certainly no wisdom or courage. Similarly, the tactics of the terrorists in the FLQ are, to put it mildly, immature. But whether the mixture of negligence and overreaction that countered them was mature or not is a much more dubious question.

We have to conclude, it seems to me, that there are no mature people. Maturity is not a thing you find in people; it's a thing that you find only in certain mental processes. These mental processes are what the university is all about: the mental processes of reason, as distinct from rationalization; of experiment; of considered evidence; of the precise and disciplined imagination that appears in literature and the arts. These processes are the end and aim of the right kind of habit, the practice-habit on which all civilized life is founded.

We think a good deal about freedom in terms of an antithesis between what the individual wants and what society will allow him to have. We tend to think of society, therefore, as inherently repressive, and we consequently have the greatest difficulty in trying to work out the conception a free society. This antithesis of freedom and compulsion is something that, as soon as we get into the mental processes I just mentioned, completely disappears. If an artist is painting a picture, what he wants to do and what he must do are the same thing. If a thinker says, "After considering this evidence, I am forced to the following conclusion," he does not mean that he is being externally compelled. The authority that compels him does not counteract his freedom: it fulfills his freedom, and it is the same thing as his freedom.

In later life one speaks of the great changes that one has lived through, usually congratulating oneself on one's power of surviving them. Certainly the changes that anyone of my age has gone through are considerable. A quarter of a century ago, the King of England was Emperor of India; Nazi Germany ruled Europe from the Atlantic to the Volga; China was a bourgeois friend; Japan a totalitarian enemy; and so on. The moral that one ought to draw from this is that what appears to be real society is not real society at all, but only the transient appearance of society. The permanent form of human society is the form that can only be studied in the arts and the sciences. Those are the genuinely organized structures of human civilization. It is in the arts and the sciences that we understand where the causes are that make society change so rapidly and seem so unpredictable. If that is true, then our definition of education has to be very different from the one that we often give. Of all the superstitions that have bedeviled the human mind, one of the most dismal and fatuous is the notion that education is a preparation for life. It was very largely this notion of education that caused the projecting of anxiety and the fear of change on the "adolescent", and on efforts to maintain him in an imaginary state of innocence.

There are two forms of society, we said, the temporary and transient appearance of society that comes to us through newspapers and television, and the real structure of society that is revealed by the arts and the sciences. Education, therefore, should be defined as the encounter with real life, whereas the world that involves us as citizens and taxpayers and readers of papers and people with jobs is not real life but a dissolving phantasmagoria. Of course, it is possible that this encounter with real life can go to the point of making one maladjusted to the dissolving world. This is, in fact, one of the functions of education. The last thing that education ought to try to do is to adjust anybody to the appearance of a society which will not be there by the time he has become adjusted to it. But it can and should make one to some extent maladjusted. In T. S. Eliot's phrase, "Human kind cannot bear very much reality", but without the little it can bear it cannot bear the rest of life.

Because of the traditional view, and for many historical reasons, university students have all been drawn from one age group, and hence they naturally assume that the university belongs to them. Actually the university belongs to the whole community, and I wish very much that this could be reflected in the make-up of the student body in the university. I am not speaking of adult education: I am speaking of a full reentry into the university by people in their thirties and forties and fifties, teachers who need refresher courses in their profession, business men who need refresher courses outside their profession, married women with grown-up families, and many other people who have had some earlier encounter with the university, but have forgotten the content of what they have learned and recognize that they need a recurrent contact with it as their life goes on. The only real reason for wanting this is the inherent worth of the subjects themselves, but there are economic advantages as well. It would be a little easier to sell education to the taxpayer if he had some sense of personal contact with it and did not feel that he was supporting only a leisure class of young people.

This conception, of the university student body as a leisure class, is a survival of an older form of social elitism. A generation ago there were fewer students in universities: it did not follow, however, that those who were there were all highly intelligent. It followed, rather, that those who were there were people of good intelligence who belonged to the middle class. A century ago the goal of university education was defined by Newman as, in the broadest sense, a social goal with the function of producing in society what Newman called the "gentleman". But it is clear that "gentleman" is no longer a socially functional conception, and the notion of the "best" education as being only the kind that the university confers is obviously a considerable social nuisance in our day.

I have taught relatively few older people in universities. I remember, however, a class in Shakespeare in which there was one man of about fifty. We were discussing *Measure for Measure* and the complicated character of its heroine Isabella. He came up to me afterwards and said, "You know, I couldn't say this in front of the class, but they all think Isabella is a grown woman, and she's not. She's a teenager. Look at the way she's crazy to go into a convent. You know, they all go through that stage." I thought that this was a fresh and candid comment on *Measure for Measure,* and I could understand why he communicated it to me in this confidential way. But it seems to me that if his age group had been more fairly represented in the class, there might perhaps have been a more understanding discussion between the two groups about what "teenagers" thought and why.

One reason why I feel the university should be deeply concerned with the education of older people is that so much technical training has such a short life, including the training of teachers and whatever undergraduate training one may have had thirty years back. It is not always understood that the research training in university graduate schools can go out of date just as quickly. As a colleague of mine remarked to me of another colleague's book, "You know, that book would have been pretty radical if he had written it one hundred years ago." The university has to be a mixture of teaching and research functions, and the two functions have constantly to update each other. A teacher who is not a scholar is soon going to be out of touch with his own subject, and a scholar who is not a teacher is soon going to be out of touch with the world.

I have referred to a kind of social elitism that still persists in our society after it has become functionally obsolete. We speak, for example, of "only a few" being capable of doing university work, and forget that, in a world as populous as ours, "only a few" can still mean a great many million. Then again, there is the mystique, as I might call it, of the small staff/student ratio. On the part of students, the belief that education is always better when there are very few students to one instructor, and when there is greatest freedom and variety of choice, is a false analogy with participatory democracy. On the part of the staff, it is a survival of the notion that teaching is an evil necessary to support research, that one's ambition ought to be to teach one's specialty, and that the fewer students you have, the higher your status ought to be. Both of these are leisure-class attitudes. It seems to me that all subjects of research do not necessarily have to be taught, and I should think that there would be many pedagogical advantages in a drastic simplification of the curriculum. Here again, though the pedagogical reasons are the only important ones, there would be economic fringe benefits, as simplifying the curriculum is the only real way to save money in higher education.

As for small classes, the tutorial system is of course greatly admired, especially by those who have never been exposed to it. But the tutorial system with all its virtues cannot give a panorama or perspective as a lecture can do. There is the corresponding mystique of the seminar. The seminar certainly has a central place in education, and should be there, and very prominently there, from the age of twelve to the time of the Ph.D. At the same time, students expect and ought to get something better from their tuition fees than merely the sound of their own ignorance coming back from the four walls. The development of fluency is also an ambiguous benefit. I have known graduates of several colleges in the United States that made a special technique of dealing with very few students at a time and teaching them to talk by means of seminars, and the echo of their horrid articulateness still rings in my ears. It seems to me that nobody should be trained to talk unless he is simultaneously trained to listen, because, if he is, then what is called "dialogue" simply becomes a series of solipsistic monologues, and any gathering of people will take on that form of group psychosis that can be studied in almost any conference called in the modern world. As for the analogy from democracy, the essential democratic principle in education is the supremacy of the subject over both the teacher and the student, and the more supreme it is, the more the difference between the teacher and the student is minimized. The implementation of democracy in the classroom comes from the teacher's willingness to share his knowledge and the student's willingness to acquire it, and the authority of the subject corresponds to the authority in democratic society of (if you will pardon what is by now a somewhat coarse expression) law and order.

If the teaching and learning conditions of the university approached at all to the conditions I have outlined, I should like to see them extended further and further down into the school program. I am aware that young children go through different stages, and we need the research of Piaget and others to tell us what those stages are and to allow for them in our teaching program. But I have invariably found that, of the teachers that I have talked to, those who most obviously knew what they were doing were also those with the least sense of difference between what they were doing and what I was doing. The same thing is true of students. Anybody who wants a substitute mother in grade two will still be wanting one in second year university.

Throughout my professional career, I have noted that teachers are occupationally disposed to believe in magic, that is, to believe in the virtues of a planned and sequential curriculum. I share that: I believe in such magic as firmly as any other teacher, and I have done a good deal of work on trying to plan sequential programs in English from kindergarten to graduate school. Teachers, at least in previous years, used to do a great deal of conferring, asking one another whether a course would not be magically improved if, instead of the sequence a, b, c, d, one had the sequence a, d, b, c, or possibly a, c, d, b. The role of the student in all this was assumed to be roughly what Newman described in his famous hymn, "Lead Kindly Light": "I loved to choose and see my path, but now lead thou me on." Newman, however, was talking to God, who is presumably a more reliable conductor than most teachers. Students have to choose and see their path, even though most of what they see is simply the consequences of choice. The teacher, in his turn, needs to realize that a teacher cannot be taught to teach except by good students. By that I do not mean such things as student evaluation, which is a parody of the genuine process, and is something for which I have no respect whatever. Rather, I am referring to a constant participation in the learning operation.

The increase of student representation on curricular and administrative bodies in the university is a part of the social life of our time, and no reasonable person is likely to oppose it. And yet, because student representation falls into the rhythm of society's movement, it tends to fall under the law of reversal that I have already mentioned. That is, as students and junior faculty become increasingly represented in a department, the department becomes so huge and cumbersome that eventually an executive committee is assigned the whole responsibility, and so the university, instead of becoming less bureaucratic and less impersonal, steadily becomes more so. It does not follow that we ought to try to reverse the trend to student and junior faculty representation, which would be futile nonsense. But in proportion as department and senate and council meetings become sounding-boards for professional noisemakers, and the running of the university is taken over by an increasingly invisible civil service, the real teachers and the real students will have to get together on a largely conspiratorial basis, forming small groups to discuss problems of primary interest to themselves. This conspiratorial activity will be what will rebuild the university.

At the University of Toronto there used to be a distinction between a three-year general course and a four-year honor course, but this has recently been swept away in a great wave of exuberant hysteria. The theories of these two courses were complementary. The theory of the general course assumed a certain coordination of disciplines, so that the student could see a broad area of knowledge from different points of view. The principle of the honor course was that every area of knowledge is the center of all knowledge. Both these theories may have required too much sophistication from both students and teachers, but I would hope that after the dust settles and the University becomes restructured, it will become restructured along the older patterns.

I am often asked if a student today is different from his predecessors, and usually the answer expected is yes. The answer happens to be no. There has been a tremendous increase in the rain of sense impressions from the electronic media, and this has produced a considerable alertness and power of perception on the part of students. However, the power to integrate and coordinate these impressions is no greater than it was. This situation has been interpreted by my colleague, Professor Marshall McLuhan, but I would regard his interpretation, if I have understood it correctly, as quite different from mine. He distinguishes between the linear and fragmented approach — which he associates with the printed book — and the total and simultaneous response, which he associates with the electronic media. It seems to me, on the other hand, that it is the existence of a written or printed document that makes a total and simultaneous response possible. It stays there: it can be referred to; it can become the focus of a community. It is the electronic media, I think, that have increased the number of linear and fragmented experiences — experiences that disappear as soon as one has had them — and with that bombardment the media have increased the general sense of panic and dither in modern society. At the same time, there is no doubt that television and the movies have developed new means of perception, and that they indicate the need for new educational techniques which, as far as I know, have not yet been worked out. I did hear a lecture some time ago by an educator that began with the showing of a television commercial. He then said, "There is one thing in that commercial which all of you missed and which all the young people to whom it was shown got at once." I thought to myself, Now we're getting to something important. Now we shall find out how education is going to adjust itself to this situation. But, unfortunately, all he said after that was, "This indicates a fact of great educational importance. We don't quite know what it is, but we have it under close study."

I have referred to the mental processes of the university as consisting of a group of things: experiment, evidence, reasoning, imagination. It is possible for different aspects of these to get out of proportion. In our day there is a tendency for one's social vision to get drowned in facts. We look at poverty and inflation and unemployment, and we feel that we can only deal with these things after we have got enough facts about them. And so we employ commissions to spend years and millions of dollars on reports, while poverty and inflation and unemployment placidly continue to rise every month. That is a disease of our time. At other times facts get squeezed out by speculative theories. Thus in the fifteenth century, for example, there was an elaborate classification of the nine orders of angels, but no classification of rocks or geological strata. The proportioning of these things results from the kind of social vision that a community has; and the university in its totality, that is, the arts and sciences taken together, defines this social vision. It is the university's task to define the vision of society. To implement that vision is the business of concerned organizations, like churches, pressure groups, and political parties. It is not the business of the university as such. In this neofascist age, there are many who dislike the kind of freedom the university represents, and would like to kidnap the university by a pressure group of some kind, radical or established, according to their prejudices. But, if this happened, society's one light would go out.

I can best conclude by trying to amplify and emphasize this point. Of course I should be cutting the throat of my own argument if I were to say that the university should be protected by and subordinated to society, because that would be putting the university in exactly the same position that I have said women were in in Victorian times and adolescents in this century. If that happened the logical result would be the spread of an ethos of Olympian indifference in which the answer to every problem would be, "Well, we'll have to wait and see until we have considered all the evidence." There is a good deal of this attitude around already, but when universities foster it they are, like the pure Victorian maiden or the bumptious contemporary adolescent, merely helping to dramatize a foolish role that society need never have invented in the first place.

The university belongs to its society, and the notion of the autonomy of the university is an illusion. It is an illusion that one would have difficulty sustaining on the campus of the University of Toronto, situated as it is between the Parliament Buildings on one side and an educational Pentagon on the other, like Samson between the pillars of a Philistine temple. But the university has a difficult and delicate job to do: it is responsible to society for what it does, very deeply responsible, yet its function is a critical one, and it can fulfil that function only by asserting an authority that no other institution in society can command. It is not there to reflect society, but to reflect the real form of society, the reality that lies behind the mirage of social trends. It is not withdrawn or neutral on social issues: it defines our real social vision as that of a democracy devoted to ideals of freedom and equality, which vision disappears when society is taken over by a conspiracy against these things. It may be attacked from the "left", as it is when certain types of radicals demand that every professor should be, in theory, opposed to war and imperialism and laissez-faire, and, in practice, a Marxist stooge. It may be attacked from the "right", as it was recently by a Toronto newspaper which, seeing a bandwagon rolling by, printed an article asserting that professors ought to be teaching students rather than subjects (perhaps the silliest of all fallacies in a subject already full of them), and reinforced this with a snarling editorial saying that professors had better reform themselves along these lines, but quick, or else "society" would do it for them. These attacks have in common the belief that "academic freedom" is an outmoded concept, dating from a time before "society" realized how easily it could destroy everything of any value. The university has to fight all such attacks, and in fighting them it becomes clear that the intellectual virtues of the university are also moral ones, that experiment and reason and imagination cannot be maintained without wisdom, without charity, without prudence, without courage; without infinite sympathy for genuine idealism and infinite patience with stupidity, ignorance, and malice. Actually, academic freedom is the only form of freedom, in the long run, of which humanity is capable, and it cannot be obtained unless the university itself is free.

JEAN VANIER

Director, L'Arche, Trosly-Breuil, France

EDUCATORS AND THE MENTALLY DEFICIENT

I want to tell you a few stories about the people who come to L'Arche, a home for handicapped adults, where I live.

With these men, we have developed a number of "tests" for visitors — "normal people" — by which we categorize them. First, there are the benevolent people who send television sets that don't work or shoes with holes in them. As they say, "I am sure that they will at least be useful to you." These are the people who, while one is sitting with Pierrot, will turn their eyes toward heaven and say, "Oh, how devoted you are!" This is a slap in the face for Pierrot. It is strange the number of people who come and visit us with this highly paternalistic, pitying attitude that is deeply wounding: deeply wounding because the handicapped person does not want pity. He wants somebody to respect him. He wants somebody to understand him. He has had enough of people who blubber over him, who give him a lot of things — television sets that don't work — but who don't believe in him.

It is always interesting to see the kinds of gifts people give and the ways in which they give them. These aspects of giving often reveal what people believe to be the quality of the man to whom they are giving the gift. For instance, there is the inflection in the voice. The "tests" we have done at L'Arche show that it is more or less normal if you do this: When you go into the workshops and are introduced to the person who is in charge, you shake hands and say "Hello" in rather a deep voice. Then, if you turn to Raphael, who is working at mosaics, or to one of the other fellows, you will say "Hello" in a high voice. It's interesting to try to diagnose the difference between the two hellos. Everybody does this; that is, if you are normal you do it. The frightening thing is, when you become aware of it, that you begin to discover that it can be a terrible thing to be normal.

I'll tell you a story that happened not too long ago when I visited a psychiatric hospital. At the far end of the hospital was the chronic ward. As we went through the building, we went first to the wards where people were ready to return to the world of normality. Apparently, they were nearly cured. They were working at desks and as we went by we would say "Hello" and they wouldn't look up. They were soon to enter into the normal world. Then we went deeper and deeper into the world of the chronic mental sickness and mental retardation till we came to the last ward. As we walked in, they would come up to us and say, "My name is John." And I would say, "My name is John, too. Isn't that great?" Then we would really get into deep and interesting dialogue because there were no barriers. It was very simple and easy. Then as we came back gradually toward the normal world, at the last ward we would say "Hello" and maybe someone would look up. Finally, we had to go back into the normal world where people just don't look at you at all.

The frightening thing is the difficulty we normal people — or at least some of us — have in relating as people, as John and Peter, as two people meeting and communing, sharing their sufferings and their joys, not afraid to show their weaknesses, not always pretending to be someone or hiding behind the barriers of position, diplomas, knowledge. All those various forms of escapism keep us from meeting our fellow men and so frequently stifle the call to compassion that is in our hearts. In reality, we are all little children. We are all little children who are weak, because metaphysically each one of us is called to death. We are weak in knowledge. We are weak in every way. We might have some passing position or knowledge, but deep in our hearts there is the quest of love and the quest to be loved. There is the quest of innocence, the desire to admire the world of flowers and stars and birds. Deep inside each one of us there is this call to innocence, by which we desire to live in a world of peace, not in a jungle.

There is also a quest for compassion, to give compassion, to understand people, and to fathom the sufferings of our fellow man. I personally do not believe that the child begins his life in a selfish way and then gradually becomes more and more oblatory. I believe that man begins as a tiny child who is in a state of "fusion" with his mother and shares in life with her. Then gradually he separates himself from the mother and turns toward objects, maybe out of frustrated love or for some other reason that I have not yet fathomed. He turns toward objects that he wants to possess and there arises in him, because of this deep frustration, the quest for possession. And with the quest for possession arises aggressiveness, in the defense of possessions. These possessions might be exterior – wealth or objects – or interior – renown, ambition, domination.

Gradually, the heart of man becomes hard and he flees this call to compassion and throws himself into a search for wealth and power and domination. His heart becomes hardened. He becomes a person who is racist, seeking segregation and division, and quickly he becomes a man who despises. He despises those who are a threat to his existence because of their color or intelligence, or because they are handicapped, or they belong to another political party or religion or philosophy. He tends quickly to despise. Then he categorizes people. He calls them "deficient" or "black" or "white" or "alcoholics" or God knows what, and he can see them only through the categories that he has created. He no longer sees Peter, or Paul, or Elizabeth. He sees a mental deficiency or a handicap, and he is rendered incapable of feeling the deep call-cry-need of the person in front of him.

A man, in order to enter into our society, with all that is needed to fulfill one's place — position, friends, diplomas, money — gradually loses his capacity for intuition. As his desire to gain and to possess and to acquire increases, there arises ever more markedly an agressiveness to defend: to defend himself, to defend his wealth. Gradually, he becomes a person of violence. Violence can take multiple forms. There is the violence of the man who looks down upon, wounds, and pushes down the despised person. You find this form of despisement in people's attitudes toward the handicapped. It can take exterior forms in which the handicapped person is actually pushed down, or it can take another form of violence which, for me, is sometimes worse: the violence of the goodwilled people who give the television set that does not work, or who dole out pity to those who need respect — respect for their right to work, their right to medical care, their right to spiritual help. This is the violence of the person who comes to the educator and says, in front of a handicapped man, "How devoted you are!"

These forms of violence are also a defense against this inner person, this weak person that is found in each one of us. We are so frightened to show our real person that we hide ourselves behind barriers of position and wealth and social standing and knowledge and diplomas. All of these constitute a hierarchy that prevents us from living fraternally. And so it is that visitors come to us at L'Arche and often are incapable of relating, incapable of listening, incapable of calling forth.

Another type of person who comes to us, similar to the benevolent one, is the specialist. Here is an example. Someone from one of the schools of special education in Paris telephoned to arrange a visit. These people were very interested in mental deficiency and wanted to visit L'Arche (if one is going to get a diploma, he should at least have seen one such community). So they rang up and said that they were very keen to visit our establishment because they had heard a lot about it. They also said that they wanted to see me because they had some special questions to ask. I said, "What sorts of questions?" And they said that they were very keen to know about the sexual problems of our men. So I said that I would be very happy to see them because I was particularly interested in the sexual problems of special educators. The poor girl who was on the other end of the phone gulped and, I imagine, wondered who this pernicious director was. I said, "We have no guinea pigs here and I have no intention of discussing the sexual problems of our men." It is like going into a family home and saying, "Tell me all about the sexual problems of your children. I am sure they must have some."

The specialist always risks falling into a trap in which knowledge clouds compassion. Often he is interested in the problems of people, but not in the people themselves. He is interested in the handicap, but not in the handicapped; in the sickness, but not in the sick person. This happens frequently with specialized people, but not always. Specialties can be a flight from compassion, but they can also be a flight to compassion, a search for greater efficacy in compassion. They can be an attempt to really help and heal the person.

Sometimes, a specialist, when he is confronted with someone who is difficult, will immediately ask to see the file because the file provides him with security. But the problem for anyone who is called to be with the handicapped is to meet the person, to look at the person, to love the person, and to see in the depths of his being the positive qualities that exist in him — qualities of simplicity, authenticity, truth — to see in him the child who is always present and who is frequently hidden under a tortured body, hidden under the wounds inflicted by a society that has made us flee from childhood. That is why I say, to those who ask for the file, "Meet the person." Once you have met the person, once you have heard his call, even though it might come through a language that you cannot yet understand, it might then be important for you to understand his past and his problems.

There is another type of person that comes to L'Arche, like the gentleman who seemed very sad and appeared to have many problems. He came to see me, and while we were talking he happened to see Jean Claude. Jean Claude is quite a character. Some people call him mongoloid, but we just call him Jean Claude. Jean Claude laughs quite a bit. He is gay. During this man's visit, Jean Claude was singing. Suddenly this man, who looked so profoundly sad, turned to me and said, *"C'est quand même terrible."* "It's terrible, isn't it, poor little fellow." How fantastically ironic, I thought, that this man who was so wrought with problems could find sadness in this little fellow who could only laugh. I wondered why he thought it was so sad. Eventually, I came to the conclusion that he was jealous. "Normal" people risk being jealous of "mad" people. Mad people have a freedom that we do not have. If you are mad you can do all sorts of eccentric things, and the psychiatrist will say, "It's in the book. The manual says on page 152 that's just how it is." He can do all sorts of things. He can jump and dance and take off his clothes. It is all really *prévu.* But we can't do that. We are condemned to live with social convention.

We have to delve into the conscience of our society. We have to ask ourselves why we have created the situations we have created for the handicapped: the psychiatric ward I described. We also have to delve into the unconscious of our society, into the motivation that has brought about this condemnation and made us lock these people up. We react in this condemnatory way with a purity of conscience that is alarming, good people that we are. Beware of good people. It is fantastic the way we can hurt people with a benevolent smile. We have to ask why is it we have such difficulty relating to those who are handicapped. Why am I so fearful, and how is it that I have closed my heart to compassion?

I like sometimes to wonder why, in the parable of the good samaritan, the levite and priest cross to the other side of the road — why each one of us crosses to the other side of the road. I suppose one of the reasons is that we have an appointment. We have created our lives around appointments. Our lives are so busy that we no longer have the time to stop on the road and to look at our handicapped brother. Why do we have so many appointments? Why are we so busy? Why have we no time to meet this person who talks so badly? Why have we no time just to listen and welcome? Because we have made ourselves and our lives so busy. We have flown from compassion. I suppose also that we must cross to the other side of the road because if we stop and look at somebody who is suffering — the handicapped or someone else — and if we are imprudent enough to start a conversation, then we risk getting involved. It's a terrible thing when you begin to identify with people in suffering.

We know that if a friend whom we loved deeply were dying of starvation, we would be unable to eat normally. We know that if the home of our parents had burned and they were in the streets, we could not sleep. So, we have to beware because as soon as we begin to identify with people who are suffering, then we are going to begin to assume that suffering into our own bodies. It cannot be otherwise. Some people who have lost hope, who are at the bottom of the pit and in the dregs of misery, will not rise up unless they feel that somebody identifies with them and is really concerned about them — not only concerned but deeply confident that they will rise up. Somebody must believe in them. It is this very belief, this desire, this hope, this identification that is the beginning of life and the rising of a new hope in the miserable person.

Yet, if we do begin to identify with others, we know full well that we shall be pulled away from the securities of our own existence. All of us tend to create a style of life that is surrounded by security that diminishes any form of anguish, a world that we can predict and prepare for day by day. We create a style of life in which we know how people are going to act and react. We create strong defenses. These are our security, manifest in wealth, friends, position — all of which separates us from the risk of identifying with the impoverished person. As soon as I become identified, really identified, with someone, *c'est que je suis pris dans les tripes.* My time, my possessions, my mode and form of life, I know, will be changed because I cannot continue to live in my particular situation when I know that you are in your suffering. And I fear the loss of my security.

I wonder why we are so frightened of losing the security of wealth and possessions and social convention and the customary mode of existence with friends. Friends can be most wonderful; they can help me and open me to the sufferings and injustices of the world, open me to mankind. But friends can also be the club of mediocrity in which we flatter ourselves, in which all we do is maintain one another in a closed society.

In point of fact, our hearts are called to universal compassion. It is true that when you meet someone in misery, if you feel called to identify yourself with him, you begin to feel dispossessed. It is a frightening experience.

I recently had the opportunity to speak to some four or five hundred convicts. It was the first occasion that I have had to speak to such men. I was deeply impressed by the quality of their listening, the quality also of their suffering. Our fear of those who are in prison begins to seem senseless once you have visited a prisoner. If you begin to meet him and meet him at a certain depth, you begin to understand that maybe it wasn't really his fault. The environmental circumstances, his family life, his suffering were all real causes of the activities that brought him to judgment and to prison. As you begin to understand the suffering and the wounds that were caused by society and by poverty and by lack of understanding, then you understand also how tortured he must be because he sees so many wealthy people throwing away money, while his own friends may be in squalor. These are the inequalities of life, of opportunity, of wealth. Some are starving, others are opulent. It is understandable that the prisoner gets angry. It is even understandable that he commits a crime.

As you enter into this understanding of the motivations of his actions and begin to suffer with him, you realize that you cannot remain the same. You realize, as you are pulled into situations and relationships, that you cannot remain a passive member of a society that permits such inequalities. So, you become more and more committed and begin to lose your friends, who haven't followed the same route as yourself, and they are left behind, often with regret. But we have to be faithful to our own call. We begin to lose interest in what interested us before and we feel some impoverishment. Then gradually we discover that we are called into another world.

These are some of the fears that prevent us from being committed. But what we want, what the handicapped want, what the marginal want, are people who are committed. Too many keep, or want to keep, their feet in both worlds. But the shoe of the opulent society is slightly bigger and wider than the other shoe, and we remain more in the world of opulence than in the world of compassion and identification. So the world goes on, divided.

I recently returned from India, a fantastic country where the eyes of the children are so bright. Fantastic eyes, the children of India! Fantastic culture! Much suffering, but a fantastic culture! In the West we tend either to minimize India and see it as a country of misery, of which we have a horror, or else to idealize it into a country of swamis and mystics whom we hope to find on every corner. The reality is neither. It is a culture. It is a civilization. It is a people who have a vision of life. A vision of time and space and people. Perhaps there is an overemphasis on non-efficacy. But there is something else: a culture, a vision of man and of life.

One goes to that fantastic land where there is much poverty, much simplicity, much politeness, and a way of sitting, a dignity. In our home in Bangalore, you would meet Gurunathan, a very Orthodox Hindu who has great dignity, shown in the way he carries his body, the way he sits, the way he smiles.

Then you would leave the Indian culture and go to Paris. It would be Christmas time, with over-lit streets and shops filled with luxury goods. The wastage! One wonders how it could be so: on one side so much simplicity and dignity, and on the other so much wastage and luxury and opulence; perhaps also so much sadness, such flight from love and life.

Compassion may be dying, and with compassion the person. It is like leaving the mental hospital where we saw eighty wonderful men, capable of relating and of easy laughter, and coming into our materialistic, fast-moving society. One wonders, where is sanity? And as one comes close to people and identifies with them, one tends to become a bit angry — maybe not angry, maybe sad. What can we do in a society that tends in so many ways to stimulate the thirst for abstract knowledge and books, but frequently, so frequently, closes its heart to people?

Suddenly, I become aware of this strange cycle of existence. If I am to identify with Raphael and Gurunathan, and with those others in the mental hospital and the prison, I should also identify with the kind lady who offered me the five pairs of shoes with the holes in them, or the lady who gave the television set that didn't work, who is living in our opulent society and is perhaps more handicapped than the fellow in the psychiatric hospital. How can I be angry with her? Maybe she, too, is just a product of our world and of her environment. If all men are our brothers, then those who are opulent are, also. Yet, what to do? They have such difficulty in relating, on the one side, a world that is crying for compassion and, on the other, a world that is fleeing from compassion. Frightened of compassion. Frightened of being hurt. Maybe frightened of dying, for perhaps in death we find life.

This is our world that continues. The handicapped continue in the psychiatric hospital. They continue not to find the homes to which they have the right, or the work they should receive, or the help and encouragement they need. And the opulent continue. This is the world that you and I are called to bring peace to. And if we do not, we shall fail seriously in our mission.

This is one of the difficult missions of anyone who calls himself an educator, or who wishes in some way to be an educator although he knows that he is the first in need of being educated. He is called to give hope to the afflicted, to look at them with eyes that call them forth to hope. He stands between them and our frightened society that clutches its securities of wealth and health and time and space and walls and rooms like little square boxes. The educator stands between these worlds and calls the afflicted to hope, calls those who are trapped in the boxes of security to open their doors, tells them not to fear. If you share your time and wealth and position and education, if you open the doors of your person without fear, then you will lose the deep fear that is at the depths of your being. You will open your gates to joy, to peace.

Peace comes not by giving superfluous goods, but by sharing. Sharing what I have. Sharing my knowledge. Not teaching, sharing. Not giving, but sharing. I give, but I also receive. I receive your smile. I receive your words. I receive your expression, your being, into my being. Maybe your smile, your unexpressed words that flow through your face and hands, your eyes that light up, perhaps these will be the keys to unlock some of the doors that I have closed around myself. It is your childlike laughter that encourages me in some little way to share; it is your laughter that will pierce the depths of my being and break down some of the barriers that I have built around myself through fear. So it is that if I continue to share without fear, those gleaming eyes and smiles and hands will continue their surgical operation in me and gradually, peacefully, tenderly will destroy those barriers of egoism that are called acquisition and property, and make of me a new man capable of sharing and calling forth the afflicted, the handicapped, and the opulent, to open the doors of our hearts toward compassion. Thus, together, we can build a world of peace, a garden and not a jungle.

IVAN ILLICH

Centro Intercultural de Documentación
Cuernavaca, Mexico

THE DE-SCHOOLING OF SOCIETY

Schools are losing their claim to a monopoly on education. The evident bankruptcy of schools, their inability to live up to their promise, is forcing educators and their clients to look beyond their mutual frustration. Within the next few years, both the purveyors and the consumers of packaged education will have to acquiesce to the end of the age of schooling, just as they have acquiesced to the end of the age of the monarchy and of the church, and teachers will have to accept a fate similar to that which befell priests and nobles in other times.

Post-scholastic consciousness is bound to appear suddenly, unexpectedly, as changes happen in a whirlpool. I remember, as a child, standing on a bridge and thinking that I would see how the whirlpool's pattern changed. I never saw it. Winter and summer it was the same. Then, one stone would fall into the basin and the whole pattern would change from one moment to another. This is the way someone falls in love, the way social consciousness changes. The consciousness of what has happened to schools will be as surprising to us as was the removal of the altar and the throne from the center of the stage of Western society.

The vision of an emerging pattern threatens the reality

of today, especially when this emerging pattern is destined to become the common sense of tomorrow. What we presently call the crisis in education is primarily the result of our attempt to make reality fit our dogma, our belief that schools are necessary. We cling to this dogma because we believe that people will not find time or motivation to learn unless they are bribed or compelled; and if we are liberals, we are convinced that the poorer a person is the more he must be bribed or compelled to submit to our educational treatment. I do believe that society can be de-schooled, that is, that we can look at what is happening at this moment in society and fit it into a pattern that does not correspond to our current ideology.

I want to distinguish my aim to de-school society from objectives of other critics of the school system who seek either to transform the world into a classroom or to establish new free schools, independent of the system. The first I would call Jacobins, the second Bourbons.

The Jacobin educator would seek to expand his right to teach everywhere. He would make us depend more on planned and engineered processes in learning, and deliver his services more persuasively through channels that touch us more intimately than a seat in the classroom, such as the mass media. He would escalate the public reliance on the knowledge industry and thereby discredit the self-learner. Having failed to make the new man by locking people provisionally into the new society, it is the logical next step for the utopian to attempt to transform society into a classroom. For the Bourbon, the present crisis in education is the result of the rude awakening of his colleague, the Jacobin, who tried to compel students to compete for a treatment that would make them equal. He wants to substitute the vulgar, universal schools of the Jacobin with more selective ones for an elite of his choosing. Many of the most articulate critics of the modern school system are, in fact, Bourbons. They are disenchanted school teachers who remain passionate educators at heart. They gain enthusiastic followings among parents and students by pointing out that schools, as they are now, do more damage than good to rich and poor alike. They demand different teachers, different rules, different kinds of community control, different curricula, different tools. Their recommendations are easily co-opted into the system of schools as soon as a foundation provides them with sufficient funds to conduct a school along their own lines, a school that is frequently more expensive than those available to everyone else. The fact that the pupils who are privileged to attend these new schools are not necessarily the rich dropouts who can afford a Summerhill — but rather an elite chosen from the poor, the blacks, the Puerto Ricans — makes it difficult for these critics to realize that they are, in reality, Bourbons.

The Jacobin utopian and the Bourbon dystopian both share the outlook of the school teacher. They seek new tools to perform their old profession. The axioms from which I start are different. I trust men to use their hearts and their brains. I want to live in a transparent society in which each moment of life is a surprising and meaningful participation in mutual education. I see human perfection in the progressive elimination of institutional intermediaries between man and the truth he wants to learn.

Schools support the claims that give professionals the power to classify people, to set the values people should have, to impose those values, and to have ultimate recourse to a science known only to them, pedagogy. The first power of the professional, to define people's needs, finds its expression in the proliferation of a school-made class system, and the subcultures of youth and childhood. It is the teacher who produces the dropout, the underdeveloped. It is the teacher who produces a particular culture of childhood and youth. As Phillipe Aries has pointed out, these are recent phenomena historically. The second power, the professional competence to declare knowledge of special value only when it has been acquired in school, trains the student in the institutionalization not only of the value of knowing but of any other value. Once I have accepted that my own learning is the result of teaching, I can accept that the acquisition of any other value is dependent on my being the client of a specialized institution. Finally, the teacher exercises the supreme authority of the professional because in the classroom he combines in himself the authority of policeman, moralist, and therapist.

Schools now serve as an overarching mechanism for a ritual that renders tolerable the fundamental contradictions within modern society. Compulsory education forces an individual to compete for equality. The myth says that we all can become equal, and the social structure says that he who consumes more does more good because he increases the flow of resources. Men learn to define what they need in terms of the goods and services large institutions like the schools can produce. They learn to define their own value in terms of their ability to consume and degrade those products, and this is as true for the socialist society of the East as it is for the consumer society of the West.

The de-schooling of society, as I conceive it, is basically a mental process, a cultural revolution. The first step must be the conviction that learning is not the result of an institutional process of teaching, and, on the part of teachers, the conviction that learning does not depend on their ability to package curricula in a particular way. The inversion of schools is primarily an attempt to get away from the notion that learning can ever be made compulsory, and to provide institutions that increase the possibility of contact between man and his environment.

A good educational system should have three purposes: it should provide all who want to learn with access to available resources at any time in their lives; empower all who want to share what they know to find those who want to learn from them; and finally, furnish all who want to present an issue to the public with the opportunity to make their challenge known. Such a system would require the application of constitutional guarantees. Learners should not be forced to submit to an obligatory curriculum or to discrimination based on possession of certificates or diplomas. The public should not be forced to support, through regressive taxation, a huge professional apparatus of educators and buildings which in fact restricts the public's chances for learning to the services the profession is willing to put on the market. Modern technology should be used to make free speech, free assembly, and a free press truly universal and, therefore, fully educational.

I believe that no more than four distinct channels or learning exchanges could contain all the resources needed for real learning. The child grows up in a world of things, surrounded by people who serve as models for skills and values. He finds peers who challenge him to argue, to compete, to cooperate, and to understand; and, if the child is lucky, he is exposed to confrontation or criticism by an experienced elder who really cares. Things, models, peers, and elders are four resources, each of which requires a different type of arrangement or network readily available to the public, and designed to spread equal opportunity for learning and teaching.

To give an example: the same level of technology is used in TV and in tape recorders. All Latin American countries have introduced TV. In Bolivia, the government has financed a TV station, which was built six years ago, although there are no more than 7,000 TV sets for four million citizens. The money now tied up in TV installations throughout Latin America could have provided every fifth adult with a tape recorder. In addition, the money would have sufficed to provide an almost unlimited library of prerecorded tapes, with outlets even in remote villages, as well as an ample supply of empty tapes. This network of tape recorders would be radically different from the present network of television. It would provide opportunity for free expression: literate and illiterate alike could record, preserve, disseminate, and repeat their opinions. The present investment in TV instead provides bureaucrats, whether politicians or educators, with the power to sprinkle the continent with institutionally produced programs which they or their sponsors decide are good for, or demanded by, the people.

The planning of new educational institutions ought not to begin with the administrative goals of a principal or president, or with the teaching goals of a professional educator, or with the learning goals of any hypothetical class of people. It must not start with the question, "What should someone learn?" but with the question, "What kinds of things and people might learners want to be in contact with in order to learn?"

Someone who wants to learn knows that he needs both information and critical response to its use from somebody else. Information can be stored in things and in persons. In a good educational system, access to things ought to be available at the sole bidding of the learner, while access to informants requires in addition others' consent. Criticism can also come from two directions: from peers or from elders, that is, from fellow learners whose immediate interests match mine, or from those who will grant me a share in their superior experience. Peers can be colleagues with whom to raise a question, companions for playful and enjoyable (or arduous) reading or walking, challengers at any type of game. Elders can be consultants with regard to which skill to learn, which method to use, what company to seek at a given moment. They can be guides to the right questions to be raised among peers, and to the adequacy or deficiency of answers arrived at.

Educational resources are usually labeled according to educators' curricular goals. I propose to do the contrary, to label four different approaches that enable the student to gain access to any educational resource that might help him to define and achieve his own goals:

(a) *Reference services to educational objects,* which facilitate access to things or processes used for formal learning. Some of these things can be reserved for this purpose, stored in libraries, rental agencies, laboratories, and showrooms like museums and theaters; others can be in daily use in factories, airports, or on farms, but made available to students, as apprentices, or during their off-hours.

(b) *Skill exchanges,* which permit persons to list their

skills, the conditions under which they are willing to serve as models for others who want to learn those skills, and the addresses at which they can be reached.

(c) *Peer matching,* a communication network that permits persons to describe the learning activity in which they wish to engage, in the hope that a partner for the inquiry can be found.

(d) *Reference services to educators-at-large,* who can be listed in a directory giving the addresses and self-descriptions of professionals, paraprofessionals, and free-lancers, along with conditions of access to their services. Such educators, as we shall see, could be chosen by polling or consulting their former clients.

Things are basic resources for learning. The quality of the environment and the relation of a person to it will determine how much he learns incidentally. Formal learning requires special access to ordinary things, on the one hand, or, on the other, easy and dependable access to special things made for educational purposes. An example of the former is the special right to operate or dismantle a machine in a garage. An example of the latter is the general right to use an abacus, a computer, a book, a botanical garden, or a machine withdrawn from production and placed at the full disposal of students.

At present, attention is focused on the disparity between rich and poor children in their access to things, and in the manner in which they can learn from them. Agencies following this approach concentrate on equalizing chances by trying to provide more educational equipment for the poor. A more radical point of departure would be to recognize that in the city rich and poor alike are artificially kept away from most of the things that surround them. Children born into the age of plastics and efficiency experts must penetrate two barriers that obstruct their understanding: one built into things, and the other around institutions. Industrial design creates a world of things that resist insight into their nature, and schools shut the learner out of the world of things in their meaningful setting.

After a short visit to New York, a woman from a

Mexican village told me she was impressed by the fact that stores sold "only wares heavily made up with cosmetics". I understood her to mean that industrial products "speak" to their customers about their allurements and not about their nature. Industry has surrounded people with artifacts whose inner workings only specialists are allowed to understand. The nonspecialist is discouraged from figuring out what makes a watch tick, or a telephone ring, or an electric typewriter work, by being warned that it will break if he tries. He can be told what makes a transistor radio work, but he cannot find out for himself. This type of design tends to reinforce a noninventive society in which the experts find it progressively easier to hide behind their expertise and beyond evaluation.

The man-made environment has become as inscrutable as nature is for the primitive. At the same time, educational materials have been monopolized by the school. Simple educational objects have been expensively packaged by the knowledge industry. They have become specialized tools for professional educators, and their cost has been inflated by forcing them to stimulate either environments or teachers.

The teacher is jealous of the textbook he defines as his professional implement. The student may come to hate the lab because he associates it with schoolwork. The administrator rationalizes his protective attitude toward the library as a defense of costly public equipment against those who would play with it rather than learn. In this atmosphere, the student too often uses the map, the lab, the encyclopedia, or the microscope only at the rare moments when the curriculum tells him to do so. Even the great classics become part of "sophomore year" instead of a new turn in a person's life. School removes things from everyday use by labeling them educational tools.

If we are to de-school, both tendencies must be reversed. The general physical environment must be made accessible, and those physical learning resources that have been reduced to teaching instruments must become generally available for self-directed learning. The use of things merely as part of a curriculum can have an even worse effect than just removing them: it can corrupt the attitudes of pupils.

The control of school over educational equipment has still another effect. It increases enormously the cost of such cheap materials. Once their use is restricted to scheduled hours, professionals are paid to supervise their acquisition, storage, and use. Then students vent their anger against the school on the equipment, which must be purchased once again.

Paralleling the untouchability of teaching tools is the impenetrability of modern junk. In the thirties, any self-respecting boy knew how to repair an automobile, but now car-makers multiply wires and withhold manuals from everyone except specialized mechanics. In a former era, an old radio contained enough coils and condensers to build a transmitter that would make all the neighborhood radios scream in feedback. Transistor radios are more portable, but nobody dares to take them apart. To change this impenetrability in the highly industrialized countries will be immensely difficult; but at least in the Third World we must insist on built-in educational qualities.

Not only the junk but also the supposedly public places of the modern city have become impenetrable. In American society, children are excluded from most things and places on the grounds that they are private. But even in societies that have declared an end to private property, children are kept away from the same places and things because they are considered the special domain of professionals and danger-ous to the uninitiated. Since the last generation, the railroad yard has become as inaccessible as the fire station. Yet with a little ingenuity, it should not be difficult to provide for safety in such places. To de-school the artifacts of education will require making the artifacts and processes available, and recognizing their educational value. Certainly, some workers would find it inconvenient to be accessible to learners; but this inconvenience must be balanced against the educational gains.

If the goals of learning were no longer dominated by schools and schoolteachers, the market for learners would be much more varied and the definition of "educational artifacts" would be less restrictive. There could be tool shops, libraries, laboratories, and gaming rooms. Photolabs and offset presses would allow neighbourhood newspapers to flourish. Some storefront learning centers could contain viewing booths for closed-circuit television; others could feature office equipment for use and for repair. The jukebox or the record player would be commonplace, with some specializing in classical music, others in international folk tunes, others in jazz. Film clubs would compete with each other and with commercial television. Museum outlets could be networks for circulating exhibits of works of art, both old and new, both originals and reproductions.

The professional personnel needed for this network would be much more like custodians, museum guides, or reference librarians than like teachers. From the corner biology store, they could refer their clients to the shell collection in the museum, or indicate the next showing of biology videotapes in a certain viewing booth. They could furnish guides for pest control, diet, and other kinds of preventive medicine. They could refer those who needed advice to "elders" who could provide it.

Two distinct approaches can be taken to financing a network of "learning objects". A community could determine a maximum budget for this purpose and arrange for all parts of the network to be open to all visitors at reasonable hours. Or the community could decide to provide citizens with limited entitlements, according to their age groups, which would give them special access to certain costly and scarce materials, while leaving other, simpler materials available to everyone.

Finding resources for material made specifically for education is only one — and perhaps the least costly — aspect of building an educational world. The money now spent on the sacred paraphernalia of the school ritual could be freed to provide all citizens with greater access to the real life of the city. Special tax incentives could be granted to those who employed children between the ages of eight and fourteen for a couple of hours each day, if the conditions of employment were humane ones. We should return to the tradition of the bar mitzvah or confirmation. By this I mean we should first restrict, and later eliminate, the disenfranchisement of the young and permit a boy of twelve to become a man fully responsible for his participation in the life of the community. Many "school age" people know more about their neighborhood than social workers or councilmen. Of course, they also ask more embarrassing questions and propose solutions that threaten the bureaucracy. They should be allowed to come of age so that they could put their knowledge and fact-finding ability to work in the service of a popular government.

Planning, incentives, and legislation can be used to unlock the educational potential within our society's huge investment in plants and equipment. Full access to educational objects will not exist so long as business firms are allowed to combine the legal protections, which the United States Bill of Rights reserves to the privacy of individuals, with the economic power conferred upon these companies by their millions of customers and thousands of employees, stockholders, and suppliers. Much of the world's know-how and most of its productive processes and equipment are locked within the walls of business firms, away from their customers, employees, and stockholders, as well as from the general public, whose laws and facilities allow businesses to function. Money now spent on advertising in capitalist countries could be redirected toward education in and by General Electric, NBC-TV, or Budweiser beer. That is, the plants and offices should be reorganized so that their daily operations would be more accessible to the public in ways that make learning possible; and indeed ways might be found to pay the companies for the learning people acquired from them.

In a world that is controlled and owned by nations and corporations, only limited access to educational objects will ever be possible. But increased access to those objects, which can be shared for educational purposes, might enlighten us enough to help us break through these ultimate political barriers. Public schools transfer control over the educational uses of objects from private to professional hands. The institutional inversion of schools could empower the individual to reclaim the right to use them for education. A truly public kind of ownership might begin to emerge if private or corporate control over the educational aspect of "things" were brought to the vanishing point.

A "skill model" is a person who possesses a skill and is willing to demonstrate its practice. A demonstration of this kind is frequently a necessary resource for a potential learner. Modern inventions permit us to incorporate demonstration into tape, film, or chart; yet one would hope that personal demonstration will remain in wide demand, especially in communication skills. Some 10,000 adults have learned Spanish at our center at Cuernavaca — most of them highly motivated persons who wanted to acquire near-native fluency in a second language. When they are faced with a choice between carefully programmed instruction in a lab, or drill sessions with two other students and a native speaker who follows a rigid routine, most choose the second.

For most widely shared skills, a person who demonstrates the skill is the only human resource we ever need or get. Whether in speaking or driving, in cooking or the use of communication equipment, we are often barely conscious of formal instruction and learning, especially after our first experience of the materials in question. I see no reason why other complex skills, such as the mechanical aspects of surgery and playing the fiddle, of reading or the use of directories and catalogs, could not be learned in the same way.

A well-motivated student, who does not labor under a specific handicap, often needs no further human assistance than can be provided by someone who is able to demonstrate on demand how to do what the learner wants to learn to do. The demand made of skilled people — that before demonstrating their skill they be certified as pedagogues — is a result of the insistence that people learn either what they do not want to know, or that all people — even those with a special handicap — learn certain things at a given moment in their lives, and preferably under specified circumstances.

What makes skills scarce or expensive on the present educational market is the institutional requirement that those who can demonstrate them may not do so unless they are given public trust through a certificate. We insist that those who help others acquire a skill should also know how to diagnose learning difficulties and be able to motivate people to aspire to learn skills. In short, we demand that they be pedagogues. Where princelings are being taught, the parents' insistence that the teacher and the person with skills be combined in one person is understandable, if no longer defensible. But for all parents to aspire to have Aristotle for their Alexander is obviously self-defeating. The person who can both inspire students and demonstrate a technique is so rare, and so hard to recognize, that even princelings more often get a sophist than a true philosopher.

Converging self-interests now conspire to stop a man from sharing his skill. The man who has the skill profits from its scarcity and not from its reproduction. The teacher who specializes in transmitting the skill profits from the artisan's unwillingness to launch his own apprentice into the field. The public is indoctrinated to believe that skills are valuable and reliable only if they are the result of formal schooling. The job market depends on making skills scarce and on keeping them scarce, either by proscribing their unauthorized use and transmission, or by making things that can be operated and repaired only by those who have access to tools or information that are kept scarce. Schools thus produce shortages of skilled persons.

Insistence on the certification of teachers is a way of keeping skills scarce. If nurses were encouraged to train nurses, and if nurses were employed on the basis of their proven skill at giving injections, filling out charts, and giving medicine, there would soon be no lack of trained nurses. Certification now tends to abridge the freedom of education by converting the civil right to share one's knowledge into the privilege of academic freedom, now conferred only on the employees of a school. To guarantee access to an effective exchange of skills, we need legislation that generalizes academic freedom. The right to teach any skill should come under the protection of freedom of speech. Once restrictions on teaching are removed, they will quickly be removed from learning as well.

The teacher of skills needs some inducement to grant his services to a pupil. There are at least two simple ways to begin to channel public funds to non-certified teachers. One way would be to institutionalize the skill exchange by creating free skill centers open to the public. Such centers could and should be established in industrialized areas, at least for those skills that are fundamental prerequisites for entrance to certain apprenticeships: such skills as reading, typing, keeping accounts, foreign languages, computer programming and number manipulation, the reading of special languages such as that of electrical circuits, the manipulation of certain machinery, and so on. Another approach would be to give certain groups within the population educational currency good for attendance at skill centers, at which other clients would have to pay commercial rates.

A much more radical approach would be to create a "bank" for skill exchange. Each citizen would be given a basic credit with which to acquire fundamental skills. Beyond that minimum, further credits would go to those who earned them by teaching, whether they served as models in organized skill centers, did so privately at home, or on the playground. Only those who had taught others for an equivalent amount of time would have a claim on the time of more advanced teachers. An entirely new elite would be promoted, an elite of those who earned their education by sharing it.

The operation of a skill exchange would depend on the existence of agencies that would facilitate the development of directory information and assure its free and inexpensive use. Such an agency might also provide the supplementary services of testing and certification, and might help to enforce the legislation required to break up and prevent monopolistic practices.

Fundamentally, the freedom of a universal skill exchange must be guaranteed by laws that permit discrimination on the basis of tested skills only, and not on the basis of educational pedigree. Such a guarantee inevitably requires public control over tests that might be used to qualify persons for the job market.

School does offer children an opportunity to escape their homes and meet new friends. But, at the same time, this process indoctrinates children with the idea that they should select their friends from among those with whom they are put. To provide the young from their earliest age with invitations to meet, evaluate, and seek out others would be to prepare them for a lifelong interest in seeking new partners for new endeavors.

A good chess player is always glad to find a close match, and one novice to find another. Clubs serve their purpose. People who want to play games, go on excursions, build fish tanks, or motorize bicycles, will go to considerable lengths to find peers. The reward for their efforts is finding those peers. Good schools try to bring out the common interests of students registered in the same program. The inverse of school would be an institution that increased the chances that persons who shared the same specific interest could meet, no matter what else they had in common.

Skill teaching does not provide equal benefits for both parties, as does the matching of peers. The teacher of skills, as I have pointed out, must usually be offered some incentive beyond the rewards of teaching. Skill teaching is a matter of repeating drills over and over and is, in fact, all the more dreary for those pupils who need it most. A skill exchange needs currency or credits or other tangible incentives in order to operate, even if the exchange itself were to generate a currency of its own. A peer-matching system requires no such incentives, but only a communications network.

Tapes, retrieval systems, programmed instruction, and the reproduction of shapes and sounds tend to reduce the need for recourse to human teachers of many skills; such equipment increases the efficiency of teachers and the number of skills one can pick up in a lifetime. Parallel runs an increased need to meet people interested in the enjoyment of the newly acquired skill. A student who has picked up Greek before her vacation would like to talk Greek when she returns. A Mexican in New York wants to find other readers of the paper *Siempre,* or of *Los Asachados,* the most popular political cartoons. Somebody else wants to meet peers who, like himself, would like to increase interest in the work of James Baldwin or of Bolivar.

The operation of a peer-matching network would be simple. The user would identify himself by name and address and describe the activity for which he sought a peer. A computer would send him back the names and addresses of all those who had inserted the same descriptions. It is amazing that such a simple utility has never been used on a broad scale for publicly valued activity. In its most rudimentary form, communication between client and computer could be done by return mail. In big cities, typewriter terminals could provide instantaneous responses. The only way to retrieve a name and address from the computer would be to list an activity for which a peer was sought. People using the system would become known only to their potential peers.

A complement to the computer could be a network of bulletin boards and classified newspaper ads, listing the activities for which the computer could not produce a match. No names would have to be given. Interested readers would then introduce their names into the system. A publicly supported peer-match network might be the only way to guarantee the right of free assembly and to train people in the exercise of this most fundamental civic activity.

The right of free assembly has been politically recognized and culturally accepted. We should now understand that this right is curtailed by laws that make some forms of assembly obligatory. This is especially the case with institutions that conscript according to age group, class, or sex, and are very time-consuming.

To de-school means to abolish the power of one person to oblige another person to attend a meeting. It also means to recognize the right of any person, of any age or sex, to call a meeting. This right has been drastically diminished by the institutionalization of meetings. Peer-matching facilities should be available for individuals who want to bring people together as easily as the village bell once called villagers to council. School buildings could often serve this purpose.

The school system, in fact, may soon face a problem that churches have faced before: what to do with surplus space emptied by the defection of the faithful. Schools are as difficult to sell as temples. One way to provide for their continued use would be to give the space to people from the neighborhood. Each could state what he would do in the classroom and when, and a bulletin board would bring the available programs to the attention of the inquirers. Access to "class" would be free or purchased with educational vouchers. The "teacher" could even be paid according to the number of pupils he could attract for any two-hour period. I can imagine that very young leaders and great educators would be the two types most prominent in such a system. The same approach could be taken toward higher education. Students could be furnished with educational vouchers that entitled them to ten hours yearly of private consultation with the teacher of their choice; for the rest of their learning, they could depend on the library, the peer-matching network, and apprenticeships.

Some who share my concern for free speech and assembly will argue that peer-matching is an artificial means of bringing people together and one that would not be used by the poor who most needed it. Some people get genuinely agitated when mention is made of creating *ad hoc* encounters that are not rooted in the life of a local community. Others react when mention is made of computerized sorting and matching of client-identified interests. People cannot be drawn together in such an impersonal manner, they say; common inquiry must be rooted in a history of shared experience at many levels, and must grow out of this experience, or in the development of neighborhood institutions, for example. I sympathize with these objections, but I think they miss my point as well as their own. In the first place, the return to neighborhood life as the primary center of creative expression might actually work against the reestablishment of neighborhoods as political units. To center demands on the neighborhood might, in fact, be to neglect an important liberating aspect of urban life: the ability of a person to participate simultaneously in several peer groups. Also, there is an important sense in which people who have never lived together in a physical community may occasionally have far more experiences to share than those who have known each other from childhood. The great religions have always recognized the importance of far-off encounters and the faithful have often found freedom through them. Peer-matching could be a significant aid toward making explicit the many potential but suppressed communities of the city.

Local communities are valuable. They are also a vanishing reality as men progressively let service institutions define their circles of social relationship. Milton Kotler has shown that the imperialism of "downtown" deprives the neighborhood of its political significance. The protectionist attempt to resurrect the neighborhood as a cultural unit only supports this bureaucratic imperialism. Far from artificially removing men from their local contexts to join abstract groupings, peer-matching should encourage the restoration of local life to cities from which it is now disappearing. A man who recovers his initiative to call his fellows into meaningful conversation may cease to settle for being separated from them by office protocol or suburban etiquette. Having once seen that doing things together depends on deciding to do so, men may even insist that their local communities become more open to creative political exchange. We must recognize that city life tends to become immensely costly as city-dwellers must be taught to rely for every one of their needs on complex institutional services. It is extremely expensive to keep it even minimally livable. Peer-matching in the city could be a first step toward breaking down citizens' dependence on bureaucratic civic services.

It would also be an essential step toward providing new means of establishing public trust. In a schooled society, we have come to rely more and more on the professional judgment of educators on the effect of their own work, in order to decide whom we can or cannot trust. We go to the doctor, lawyer, or psychologist because we trust that anybody with an amount of specialized educational treatment by other colleagues deserves our confidence. In a de-schooled society, professionals could no longer claim the trust of their clients on the basis of their curricular pedigree, or ensure their standing by simply referring their clients to other professionals who approve of their schooling. Instead of placing trust in professionals, it should be possible, at any time, for any potential client to consult with other experienced clients of a professional about their satisfaction with him, by means of another peer network easily set up by computer, or by a number of other means. Such networks could be seen as public utilities that permitted students to choose their teachers, or patients their healers.

As citizens have new choices, new chances for learning, their willingness to seek leadership should increase. We could expect them to experience more deeply both their own independence and their need for guidance. As they were liberated from manipulation by others, they would learn to profit from the discipline others have acquired in a lifetime. De-schooling education should increase rather than stifle the search for men with practical wisdom who are willing to sustain the newcomer on his educational adventure. With an increasing demand for teachers, their supply should also increase. As the schoolmaster vanishes, the conditions arise that should bring forth the vocation of the independent educators. This may seem almost a contradiction in terms, so thoroughly have schools and teachers become complementary. Yet this is exactly what the development of the first three educational exchanges would tend to produce, and what would be required to permit their full exploitation; for parents and other "natural educators" need guidance; individual learners need assistance; and the educational networks need people to operate them.

Three types of special educational competence should be distinguished: one to create and operate the kinds of educational exchanges or networks outlined; another to guide students and parents in the use of these networks; and a third to act as *primus inter pares* in undertaking difficult intellectual exploratory journeys. Only the former two can be conceived of as branches of an independent profession: educational administration or pedagogical counseling.

To design and operate the networks I have been describing would not require many people, but it would require people with the most profound understanding of education and administration, in a perspective quite different from and even opposed to that of schools. While an independent educational profession of this kind would welcome many people the schools exclude, it would also exclude many whom the schools qualify. The establishment and operation of educational networks would require some designers and administrators, but not in the numbers or of the type required for the administration of schools. Student discipline, public relations, hiring, supervising, and firing teachers would have neither place nor counterpart in the networks I have been describing. Neither would curriculum-making, textbook purchasing, the maintenance of grounds and facilities, or the supervision of interscholastic athletic competition. Nor would child custody, lesson planning, and record keeping — which now take up so much of the time of teachers — figure in the operation of educational networks. Instead, the operation of networks would require some of the skills and attitudes now expected from the staff of a museum, a library, an executive employment agency, or from a *maître d'hôtel*.

Today's educational administrators are concerned with controlling teachers and students to the satisfaction of others: trustees, legislators, and corporate executives. Network builders and administrators would have to demonstrate genius at keeping themselves and others out of people's way, and at facilitating encounters of students, skill models, educational leaders, and educational objects. Many persons now attracted to teaching are profoundly authoritarian and would not be able to assume this task. Building educational exchanges would mean making it easy for people, especially the young, to pursue goals that might contradict the ideals of the traffic manager who makes the pursuit possible.

If the networks I have described can emerge, the educational path of each student would be his own to follow, and only in retrospect would it take on the features of a recognizable program. The wise student would periodically seek professional advice: assistance to set a new goal, insight into difficulties encountered, choice between possible methods.

While educational network administrators would concentrate primarily on the building and maintenance of roads providing access to resources, the pedagogue would help the student find the path that could lead him fastest to his goal. If a student wanted to learn spoken Cantonese from a Chinese neighbor, the pedagogue would be available to judge proficiency, and to help select the textbooks and methods most suitable to the student's talents, character, and the time available for study. The pedagogue could counsel the would-be airplane mechanic as to the best places for apprenticeship. He could recommend books to somebody who wanted to find challenging peers to discuss African history. Like the network administrator, the pedagogical counselor would regard himself as a professional educator. Access to either could be gained by individuals through the use of educational vouchers.

The role of the educational initiator or leader, the master or "true" leader, is somewhat more elusive than that of the professional administrator or pedagogue. This is so because leadership is hard to define. In practice, an individual is a leader if people follow his initiative, his progressive discoveries, and become apprentices. It is hard to amplify this definition except in the light of personal values or preferences; frequently, prophetic vision of entirely new standards is involved, in which present "wrong" will turn out to be "right". In a society that would honor the right to call assemblies through peer-matching, the ability to take educational initiative on a specific subject would be as wide as access to learning itself. But, of course, there is a vast difference between the initiative taken by someone to call a fruitful meeting to discuss this paper, and the ability of someone to provide leadership in the systematic exploration of its implications.

Leadership also does not depend on being right. As Thomas Kuhn points out, in a period of constantly changing paradigms, most of the very distinguished leaders are bound to be proven wrong by the test of hindsight. Intellectual leadership does depend, nonetheless, on superior intellectual discipline and imagination, and on willingness to associate with others in the exercise of imagination and intellect.

The relationship of master and disciple is not restricted to intellectual discipline. It has its counterpart in the arts, in physics, in religion, in psychoanalysis, and in pedagogy. It fits mountain-climbing, silver-working and politics, cabinetmaking and personnel administration. What is common to all true master-pupil relationships is the awareness both share that their relationship is literally priceless and in very different ways a privilege for both.

In practice, there will always be a fuzzy line between the teacher of skills and the educational leaders identified above, and there are no practical reasons why access to some leaders could not be gained by discovering the "master" in the drill-teacher who introduces students to his discipline. On the other hand, what characterizes the true master-disciple relationship is its priceless character. Aristotle speaks of it as a "moral type of friendship, which is not on fixed terms: it makes a gift, or does whatever it does, as to a friend." Thomas Aquinas says of this kind of teaching that inevitably it is an act of love, and mercy. This kind of teaching is always a luxury for the teacher and a form of leisure (in Greek, *"scholē"*) for him and his pupil: an activity meaningful for both and having no ulterior purpose.

To rely for true intellectual leadership on the desire of gifted people to provide it is obviously necessary even in our society, but it could not be made into a policy now. We must first construct a society in which personal acts reacquire a value higher than that of making things and manipulating people. In such a society, exploratory, inventive, creative teaching would logically be counted among the most desirable forms of leisurely "unemployment".

Inevitably the de-schooling of society blurs the distinctions between economics, education, and politics on which the stability of the present world order of nation states rests. In addition to the tentative conclusions of the Carnegie Commission reports, the past year has brought forth a series of important documents showing that schooling for certification cannot continue to be counted upon as the central educational device of a modern society. Julius Nyerere of Tanzania has announced plans to integrate education with village life. In Ontario, the Wright Commission on postsecondary education has reported that no known system of formal education could provide equal opportunities for the citizens of Ontario. The president of

Peru has accepted the recommendation of his commission on education, which proposes to abolish free schools in favor of free educational opportunities provided throughout life. In fact he is reported to have insisted that this program proceed slowly at first in order to keep teachers in school and out of the way of true educators. What has happened is that some of the boldest and most imaginative public leaders have found their insights into school failures matching those of radical free spirits who, like Paul Goodman, were considered "anarchic" only a few years ago.

The alternative to social control through the schools is the voluntary participation in society through networks that provide access to all its resources for learning. In fact, these networks now exist, but they are rarely used for educational purposes. The crisis of schooling, if it is to have any positive consequence, will inevitably lead to their incorporation into the educational process.

BRUCE RUSK

Project Officer, Office of Field Development
Ontario Institute for Studies in Education

ALTERNATIVES IN EDUCATION

I am one of the lower-middle-class youth you have read about who entered teaching, seeking upward mobility and social status. But, in addition, there was a higher motive — a basic faith in the value of education, a belief that schools were instruments for the betterment of mankind and that teaching was a form of service to society.

For a long time I had known that I wanted to teach. I still remember battling with the other kids on the street to see who would be teacher when we "played" school. And when the time came to enter university and to choose a field, my reasoning went along these lines:

1. You should teach what you do well.
2. In high school, I did well at Latin and Greek.
3. Therefore, I should study Classics at university and teach Latin and Greek.

Looking back on the process, it is interesting that I had no thought of what would be exciting or challenging to communicate to others. The criteria for making a decision that governed many years of my life and stamped me with an academic identity were the criteria of performance that I had learned in the educational system.

After an M.A. in Greek and several years of teaching, I

became convinced that Classics was not relevant enough for me, that some greater social commitment was required. I became involved then in inner city work, particularly in preschool programs for the educationally disadvantaged, convinced that through equality of educational opportunity racial differences would disappear and class distinctions would be overcome. While my faith in the relevance of Classics had been lost, my basic faith in the value of education held fast.

While I can now admit that I had experienced twinges of doubt in the past, it is only recently that this basic faith in education has been openly challenged. It began when Edgar Friedenberg* delivered his talk on the abolition of the educational system at a conference I arranged. My initial reaction was confusion and outrage. But the twinges of doubt became personal issues with which I had to come to terms. It was at this point that I discovered the work of Ivan Illich and Everett Reimer and finally visited their Centro Intercultural de Documentación in Cuernavaca. In Mexico, I finally lost my faith. The faith that was lost, however, was not a faith in education, but in schooling, in the belief that learning experiences can be considered legitimate only when they take place within the institution of the school.

It was with this background that I began planning the Institute's fifth anniversary lectures — with two purposes in mind. First, I hoped to provoke others to experience the same challenge to their faith in schooling that I had so recently experienced. But also I hoped to find, if not answers to my own dilemmas, at least new directions for myself.

Whether others experienced a crisis in faith as a result of the lecture series is difficult to measure. A list of the attendance figures and a report of the press and media coverage would indicate at least that the ideas contained in

* Edgar Friedenberg, "The Student and the System" in *The Student and the System,* ed. by Bruce Rusk, Tim Hardy, and Bill Tooley (Toronto: Ontario Institute for Studies in Education, 1970).

the lectures were widely disseminated. More than 4,500 people attended the lectures. Ivan Illich's and Northrop Frye's lectures were filmed in their entirety by ETVO and television interviews were scheduled with six of the speakers. Postman's lecture was rebroadcast on CBC's *Ideas.* Several of the lectures received quite full press coverage in local papers and national press services. In addition, many tapes of the lectures have been sold.

The outcome of the second purpose is contained in a proposal for a Center in Educational Alternatives, developed with Bill Tooley and Ed Waitzer.* The proposal is based on the assumption that in an urbanized media-oriented environment the majority of most people's learning experiences take place outside the institution of the school. Up to now, the school has tried to encompass more and more of these learning experiences in order to legitimate what pupils have already learned and to make the curriculum of the school relevant. However, through this process of co-optation by the schools, learning that was once spontaneous and subconscious has become distorted and stultified, in the process of being made conscious through programming curricula.

The process of expanding the school walls has also proven too costly for both developing and developed societies. Instead of expanding the school to include more and more of the community, as Illich's Jacobins advocate, we propose to explore community resources, to inventory those that already provide learning experiences, to develop those that appear to have educational potential, and to create in the public an awareness of the legitimacy of those learning experiences for the preparation of individuals for a role in society.

Whereas the programs Illich has proposed (peer matching, skill matching, etc.) tend to match individuals with individuals, we would try to establish cooperation among

---

* Bruce Rusk, William Tooley, and Edward Waitzer, "Proposal for a Center in Educational Alternatives", brief submitted to the Commission on Post-Secondary Education, March 24, 1971.

groups and organizations in order to develop educational programs that would use community resources with more effectiveness. The individual would then be provided with information and access to these learning resources. Some programs that we would like to see developed would be concerned with language and culture, work-study, and apprenticeship.

Language and culture programs

In most Canadian cities there are ethnic organizations that provide social activities for members and frequently educational activities as well, to integrate members into Canadian society. These organizations could be encouraged to develop language and culture programs for nonmembers. This service would involve training some members of the organization in basic instructional techniques, and advertising the programs to nonmembers. Someone planning a trip to Greece, or a high school or university student, might then study Greek through programs offered at a Greek center rather than through courses in the schools. In doing so, the "student" would enter more deeply into the cultural milieu than if he were to study the language in classrooms and language laboratories. Such programs would also promote an awareness to the contribution to be made by ethnic groups to a multicultural Canadian society, both to the members of the majority cultures and to those of the various ethnic groups.

Work-Study Programs

Many community organizations have work that needs to be done. Many people want educational experiences that could be obtained more effectively through field work than through classroom instruction. Programs could be developed that would combine learning experiences, work, and community service; and individuals who wanted that kind of experience could be matched to the programs. For example, one might "study" child development or cognitive psychology while working in a day-care center. One might "study" sociology by investigating the impact of the GO transit, or urban life through the collection and analysis of questionnaires. One might "study" household economics by visiting old people or invalids and assisting them with basic household duties. Students in this type of program would not only learn skills and processes, they would also perform services that would be invaluable to the community.

Apprenticeships

The schools have gradually assumed more and more responsibility for training students in skills that are useful to industry. The result is, first, that educational costs have escalated as schools have tried to duplicate equipment available in industry; and, second, that students have emerged with dated skills acquired through programs detached from industrial development. Programs could be developed to return industrial training to industry. Industry would then be responsible for training individuals in specialized skills, as is currently the case with computer programming. These industrial programs would provide an alternative to many of the courses currently offered in vocational high schools and community colleges.

The second assumption underlying the proposal for a Center in Educational Alternatives is that change cannot be effected by lectures, or conferences, or even government commissions, but that change is effected by individuals' engaging in examined activity. After determining the needs and resources of a community and the level of interest in a particular program, the center would attempt to initiate a variety of pilot activities that would be observed during their development and evaluated after a period of time. In developing a program, the center would aim to make it independent administratively and financially. Thus, a program would be considered successful only when it passed out of the center's jurisdiction.

The purpose of the center we have proposed is not to work toward the de-schooling of society. With Illich, we assume that this process is already taking place, that schools are no longer the primary mechanism for education in an urbanized media-oriented society, and that they are a mechanism that the society cannot support much longer in their present form. Rather, the purpose of the center is to provide access to educational resources that already exist in any community, and to develop a variety of alternative approaches to education. This process would allow the schools to redefine their own role as one of the educational alternatives, to determine what can best be communicated through school instruction, and to return a considerable amount of educational responsibility to other agencies and individuals.

If this plan were to succeed, the elementary school would continue to exist, but it would concentrate on the communication of basic skills: reading, writing, arithmetic, language arts. All students would be expected to reach a high level of performance in these skills and teachers would be evaluated on the performance of their pupils. Other subjects would be introduced, but in a purely nonevaluative way. For example, students might be exposed to a range of musical traditions, but they would never be asked to answer questions such as, "I like this symphony because. . . ." To supplement the elementary school, baby-sitting services would be provided through parks and community agencies. School would be compulsory, if at all, only up to twelve years of age. After the student had completed a program in the elementary school, he would be free to choose from a range of alternative educational programs and services, some of which would be offered through the schools. However, from the time he completed his elementary program, education would be a continuing rather than a continuous process, and the individual would constantly move in and out of learning situations throughout his lifetime.

The end of the age of schooling is at hand. The questions

that remain to be answered are how long will it take us to recognize it and to provide other societal mechanisms to serve the basic human need to learn. I hope that the Province of Ontario will lead the way in dealing with these questions and that the Ontario Institute for Studies in Education will contribute to the search for solutions. These fifth anniversary lectures and their publication could then mark a stage in the creation of alternative futures in education.